Giving Children a Voice

Giving Children a Voice

The Transforming Role of the Family

Edited by

Catherine Bernard and John Shea

Cambridge Scholars Publishing

Giving Children a Voice: The Transforming Role of the Family

Edited by Catherine Bernard and John Shea

This book first published 2015

Cambridge Scholars Publishing

Lady Stephenson Library, Newcastle upon Tyne, NE6 2PA, UK

British Library Cataloguing in Publication Data
A catalogue record for this book is available from the British Library

ISBN (10): 1-4438-7045-5
ISBN (13): 978-1-4438-7045-0

To the Youth and Children of Our World

TABLE OF CONTENTS

PREFACE

The global congress on "*Giving Children a Voice—The Transforming Role of the Family in a Global Society*" was held at New Delhi, India, in January 2009. It was organized by Service and Research Institute on Family and Children (SERFAC), a nongovernmental organization based in Chennai, India.

SERFAC, previously known as Service and Research Foundation of Asia on Family and Culture, was given its present name at the congress. It enjoys Special Consultative Status with ECOSOC of the United Nations.

The congress was unique in that it brought together over 150 experts and professionals from 25 countries, and a parallel children's congress was simultaneously organized, attended by 40 child delegates drawn from 28 countries. During one panel session, the children addressed an audience of adults, making known to them their thinking and experiences, and called upon the adult world to be attentive to them and listen to what they have to say to us.

These and other moving experiences at the congress prompted us to compile papers presented there into a book to make it available to a larger audience the world over.

The papers in this volume challenge the stereotypes of what children and families are expected to be and do. They challenge society at large to note the seriousness of child abuse, and the impact of technology on children. They also raise questions on the rights of the child, and the role of parenthood in today's contexts.

The papers have been updated for this publication. This volume, I hope, will be a perennial source of inspiration to all persons who deal with children, and an excellent resource manual for those in professional practice and/or those wishing to further their research.

We at SERFAC believe that the contents of this book can and will be a potent vehicle to build a more humane, caring and technologically balanced world where knowledge sharing, coupled with delicate human love, will enrich each of us with the wisdom that holds the key to the future—this is what Family is all about. This is what children want and need. With this, the Family will become a capable institution where parents guide the young, and together they transform our globalized and globalizing world order, making it a haven of peace and security for our children.

The future of the world is in the hands of our children. Society today often fails to hear the wake-up call embedded in the happenings of the world, which in many ways is driven by technology and concerns of profit at the cost of human lives, especially the lives of children. The future is for the children of today—we need to give it to them today.

Dr. Catherine Bernard
Founder-Director, SERFAC

ACKNOWLEDGMENTS

I am grateful to the members of the Planning Committee of the Global Congress on *Giving Children a Voice—The Transforming Role of the Family*: Dr. H.B. Danesh of Canada, Prof. Victoria Thoresen of Norway, Dr. John Shea, of the US, Dr. Kim Khoo Choo of Singapore and Dr. Caroline de Leon of the Philippines, who, despite constraints of time and distance and their own commitments, met several times before the event to discuss and delve deep into the meaning and intricacies contained in the title of the congress. Their exemplary team spirit and commitment to the cause of children and family were manifest during the conduct of the congress.

I am proud to be associated with the outstanding and globally acclaimed resource persons who presented their papers and contributed to the excellent conduct of the workshops held during the congress. I am grateful to them for their contributions.

My special thanks to Ms. Karen Gonsalvez, who effectively conducted the parallel Congress for Children. The bonding that took place as the event for the children concluded was a sign of its impact, success, and meaningfulness to all.

I acknowledge with deep appreciation the support and contributions of Ms. Ann Gonsalvez, who assisted with the preparations and logistics which contributed to the successful conduct of the event.

I thank Mr. Pooran Pandey, Chief Executive of The Times Foundation, now Executive Director of Global Compact Network India, for the support and help offered for the success of the event.

Without the generous grants from the Agencies of Missio Aachen, Kindermissionswerk, Aachen and Missio Munich, all of Germany, and Holy Childhood, Rome, this Congress would not have been possible. I thank them.

To the dedicated staff of SERFAC, my sincere thanks.

To Ms. Susan Philip, for her care in editing and preparing the manuscript for printing, my special thanks.

My sincere thanks to the Cambridge Scholars Press for welcoming the proposal and publishing this book.

Dr. Catherine Bernard
Founder-Director, SERFAC

INTRODUCTION

Marking the 10th Anniversary of the International Year of The Family (IYF), the outcome document, 'A Celebration of the Family' stated: "The Family is a universal and irreplaceable community, rooted in human nature, that is the basis for all times. As the cradle of life and love for each new generation, the family is the primary source of personal identity, self-esteem and support for children. It is also the first and foremost school of life uniquely suited to teach children integrity, character, morals, responsibility, service and wisdom." (Administration for Children and Families, US Department of Health and Human Services, October 2006) The United Nations affirms that "The family provides the natural framework for the emotional, financial and material support essential to the growth and development of its members, particularly infants and children." (IYF No 18: Chapter 1, Section B-Societies and Family in Crises-No 18.October 1995, p 5)) A similar US document dated October 2004 highlighted the relationship of Marriage to Family when it stated that "Despite well-documented decline, the institution of marriage remains central to family life. Indeed, in bringing together two people in a lifelong bond, marriage creates new families. Marriage also links existing families in manners that invigorate and perpetuate both. Marriage weaves ties of belonging between the couple, their parents and extended kin, their anticipated children and society at large." (Administration for Children and Families, Department of Health and Human Services, October 2004).

While the Universal Declaration of Human Rights affirms that "men and women of full age have the right to marry and found a family," it also says that "Marriage is not so much about rights, but responsibilities. The married couple sets a pattern of sacrifice, duty and occupation that naturally flows with parental duties of raising and nurturing children." ('A Celebration of the Family'- Observance of the Tenth Anniversary of The International Year of The Family, Administration for Children and Families, US Department of Health and Human Services, October 2004 p 2 .Why Family MATTERS-The relationship of Marriage to Family)

These stark statements take the reader to the heart of this publication, which discusses the following:

1. Why Marriage and Family matter for children
2. How the Family is a microcosm of the larger world, and the impact of modern pressures on the Family
3. How parental attitudes affect children.
4. The Role of the State in supporting healthy marriages, strengthening two-parent families, and protecting children.

This book is a compilation of articles presented at the 12th International Conference and Third World Congress of the Service and Research Foundation of Asia on Family and Culture (SERFAC), Chennai, India. *"Giving Children a Voice: The Transforming Role of the Family in a Global Society"* was the theme of the conference, held in 2009.

Now, more than five years later, the issues facing children persist, and, if anything, have escalated. The contents of this book highlight the atrocities done to children. The concerns raised at the conference are even more of a reality today, and the remedial measures suggested at the conference by experts are as relevant as they were then.

The crucial ambience required for protecting the child and strengthening the voice of the child is the Family. The first chapter talks about the importance of the Family, the role it has to play in the safeguarding and development of children, and what parents can do to ensure the emergence of a responsible, well-adjusted generation.

Other chapters talk of the importance of child rights, the effects of globalization on families, the repercussions of sexual victimization of children, the stultifying impact of violence, neglect, and poverty on children, and the need for educating the adult on the tenets of responsible parenting.

The voices of eminent psychologists and sociologists working for and with children and families, heard through the following chapters, will hopefully convey to the thinking population of the 21st century, particularly the men and women who hold the responsibility of guiding the future of the world through policies and plans, that it is crucial to protect children and strengthen their voices which are often muffled or silenced by abuse, victimization, crime, domestic abuse, abandonment, poverty, labor, wars, pornography, crime, and similar atrocities.

The inherent goodness and sensitivities of children need to be captured in mature environments, be it at home, school, or workplace, and they need to be raised in a manner that allows them their childhood, their playfulness, laughter, and freedom, so as to enable an environment of identity to prevail when they reach adolescence, and maturity as they grow into adulthood.

Dr. Catherine Bernard

References

1. Developed by the Administration for Children and Families, US Department of Health and Human Services, October 2006.
2. IYF. No.18: Chapter I, Section B – Societies and Family in Crises – No. 18, 1995, p5.
3. Developed by the Administration for Children and Families, Department of Health and Human Services, in October 2004.
4. 'A Celebration of the Family'—Observance of the tenth anniversary of the International year of The Family, Developed by the Administration for Children and Families, US Department of Health and Human Services, October 2004, p 2. Why Family Matters – The Relationship of Marriage to Family.

CHAPTER ONE

SECRETS OF A HEALTHY FAMILY

CATHERINE BERNARD

Introduction

Civic and religious leaders, political philosophers, social psychologists, historians, and a host of social and behavioral scientists refer to 'Family' as the foundation of society, cornerstone of civilization, potent vehicle for the transmission of culture, seedbed of virtues, medium for fostering social cohesion and religious harmony, and so on, at every level of the human spectrum. Yet, when we look around us, we are alarmed by the increase in domestic violence, social unrest, waging of wars, disrespect for moral and legal law, and the loss of value and respect for human life. Alongside, we experience an increase in delinquency, crime, and bribery. All of today's offenders and war wagers were the children of not so long ago. For whatever reason, they are the products of improper training and education, perhaps of their generation and of generations of children before them.

They were perhaps deprived or/and stifled when they were children and now that they are adults, they are the wrong people, with the wrong voices in the wrong places, occupying wrong positions contributing to disharmony in society and the destruction of all human relationships and social safety nets, including the Family.

This Chapter—Secrets of a Healthy Family—does not ignore the risks and perils children and families face in our contemporary world. It is meant to offer a ray of hope to couples and families. Despite the unhealthy trends in society in general and nations in particular, the chapter focuses on a proactive approach and helps foster the understanding that "marriage and parenthood are unique, irreplaceable and indispensable institutions, and children are incarnations of love between husband and wife and gifts to humanity." It hopes to help readers understand the necessary environments that need to be created in the home in which children will be enabled to have a voice and exercise their voice as they grow into adulthood.

Why Marriage and Family Matter for Children

Marriage and family are the naturally created institutions that go hand in hand in establishing a family. Marriage is an incubator for personal development and socialization of children. It is an institution born out of "love," for mutual acceptance and responsible living. Marriage also provides an ambience to enjoy life and relate with other people and function well in the world. Staying married is in many ways a paradox. Marriage needs to be nurtured more than nurturing children, as it is from this stability, security and safety net that healthy parenting flows. It must also be recognised that although marriage has undergone profound changes, it continues to be the most effective family structure in which to raise children.

A stable family meets the basic needs of children. "Caring for children remains the most generally recognized basic responsibility of families, because the human infant needs a great deal of care in order to survive. Human development requires emotional involvement and interaction with the child as well as physical care." (UN IYF Occasional Papers Series 1992 No 2, *Family: Forms and Functions*). Statistics tell us that children with parents in stable marriages have more self-esteem and self-confidence, fare better in school, and are more appropriately socialized on average than children with parents in unhealthy and weak relationships.

Children in intact families spend more time with parents especially during mealtimes (evening meal most likely), compared to children from families where the husband–wife relationship is not sound. Adolescents from intact families are less likely to become addictive, sexually active, or social misfits. They are likely to have stable and healthy relationships, intact marriages, and families themselves, and are more likely to provide safe environments, healthy socialization, and nurturing homes to their children.

Children look to parents as models for security, warmth, and guidance. They learn from the father about being a man and treating women with respect, compassion and love, and being caring from the mother. Joe Beam in his article on Parenting says "Your marriage and parenting not only will help it but will also help them in the future. It will provide them a pleasant home and marriage." (Joe Beam, Marriage Helper 911). The author goes on to say "The good things in your marriage will usually trickle down to your children to come."

In brief, "in a thriving family, not only do the members get along well together, but encourage each other's accomplishments and allow each other to be successful. The mother as much as the father, the children as well as the parents, productive and confident, each family member is happy and a source of happiness for the others." (Khalil A Khavari & Sue Williamston Khavari, Creating a Successful Family).

Impact of Modern Pressures on Marriage and Family—A Microcosm of the Larger World

Families have been changing ever since they came into existence. However, we need to recognize that we live in highly stressful times with unprecedented technological change affecting every aspect of life. The sheer pace of change calls for stable and healthy families so that people have the necessary emotional strength to deal with them. Yet, when the need to rely on them is greatest, too often we find contemporary families are vulnerable, even fragile, because personal interactions between parents and between parents and children are weak, and fragmented as never before. Hence, special efforts must be made to learn, form, and maintain healthy relationships from within a stable and healthy family.

Families and individual members within a family are not isolated from each other, remote and unaffected by the society in which they live. One of the major reasons why problems arise is the failure to recognize the velocity of change in society as a whole, and how it affects relationships within the family. Some of these changes are comprehensible, some are puzzling, but all have a greater or lesser impact on us. If one were to look beyond the immediate and from a more historical perspective, it is possible to make sense of what otherwise seems to be random, oppressive and illogical events.

It must be recognized that families everywhere are strongly influenced by educational levels, industrialization, technological dominance, migration, restructuring of economies, change in global trade patterns and practices, impact of unemployment, migration, materialism, and massive changes with regard to attitudes, values, and lifestyles. These changes have, in new ways, built new walls of attitudes and lifestyles of individualism or collective insulation, while simultaneously demolishing the barriers of distance that once separated people and hindered the flow of ideas between peoples of different cultures, bringing about considerable re-routing in learning curves all through life.

In contemporary times, change, by its very nature, is aimed at undermining the stability of marriage and family life. The very existence of the Family is sought to be swept out by many. Some even question the need for marriage and the utility of the family and marital commitment to the needs of children. While there is no specific data available on divorce, there is indication that marriage rates have declined over the years with an increase in divorce rates around the world, along with a simultaneous numerical leap in unwed pregnancies and cohabitation. The consequences of these trends on the health and well-being of couples themselves and of the children and the community cannot be underestimated. These trends, which are active around the world and gaining increasing velocity in some countries, with contagious effects on others, are highly detrimental to the fulfilment of human needs, especially those of children and marriage. They call for an extremely urgent strengthening of family life and family relationships for the well-being of future generations.

Insights from research in behavioral and social sciences have influenced popular concepts of socialization and their manifold effects on adults, adolescents, and children. The current term "globalization," which has in many ways been imposed on some countries and in some ways has been unquestioningly adopted by younger generations, has led to profound differences, especially between developed and developing nations, the rich and the poor in each nation, and at micro levels, between parents and children and in our homes between our own present lifestyles and those of our elders.

Ervin Lazlo writes: "All societies in the world today are in a process of transformation. Technologies and institutions as well as values, beliefs and goals are changing." (Ervin Lazlo, *et al* (1948) *Goals for Mankind*) Change, therefore, will be the pattern of our lives and to cope effectively with it, we will have to see it in a positive light and enable children to develop resilience in order to make choices and resist the processes that are negative and/or destructive. To ignore the reality of change will only sap our energies and block our attempts to understand it.

How Parental Attitudes Affect Children

It is also in the interest of parents and society to examine their personal beliefs, perceptions, and attitudes, because they are crucial in family life and affect spousal relationship, parent–child relationships, and the way in which children are raised. Psychologists have established that expectations have an important influence on the behavior of children. If children are expected to be bad, they will be. When children are constantly told they are naughty or bad and treated with impatience, they will not have a chance to learn and develop the human values that rightfully belong to them. They may grow up lacking self-confidence, self-esteem, and social skills, and be handicapped in their relationships with others. Human behavior is largely the result of a person's will, a will that was shaped by learning from others and life's experiences. Poor behavior is not, we believe, the result of any inborn evil, but usually reflects ignorance resulting from a lack of socialization and clear guidance. To expect a child to "behave" when he or she does not know what appropriate behavior might be, is to minimize the child's voice. It is the task of the parents to assist and enable the child to speak, acquire good habits, and develop a positive character. The objective is best achieved when both parents point out the desirable from the unacceptable and encourage positive behavior in the child.

If parents believe that human beings are fundamentally good and capable of developing the higher qualities, such as kindness, they will teach their children constructive ways of dealing with life issues and expectations. Parents need to remember they are role models to show how these values can be translated into everyday living. When trusted and respected, a child will be valued as a friend and a gift.

Children need to be loved and cared for from conception to adulthood and after. Children need to enjoy warmth and enduring relationships with their parents. Where the relationship between the husband and wife is enduring, children grow up in the security of a home where values are not only taught but caught, and integrated adulthood can be expected to emerge. When parents bring to their marriage the ingredients of love, trust, and caring, they build into the relationship values that are lasting and enduring and can stand the test of time and change.

Secrets of a Healthy Family

The secrets of a healthy family are the ability of parents to listen to their children and work out with them answers to their questions and pay attention to their issues without belittling them or their experiences. Parents need to foster a positive environment in spite of change and challenges; the urgent need is to prevent problems from arising in the first place.

What Parents Can Do to Give Children a Voice

Parents must first be convinced of the innate value of the child, for it is this that makes all their efforts meaningful and worthwhile. Second, they need to improve their own frames of reference in order to become better examples. Third, there must be unity and love between parents as a married couple. Four, they must understand the developmental stages and goals of childhood.

Developmental Stages and Goals of a Child

Stage	**GOAL**
Infancy	Developing trust
Toddler	Developing independence
Pre-school age	Developing initiative
School age	Developing industry
Adolescence	Developing self-identity.

(Donna Ewy & Rodger Ewy, (1985). Preparation for Parenthood)

Each child will grow through each developmental stage at his or her own pace, regardless of what parents or siblings did at that age. Providing a nurturing environment for reasonable expectations tailored to the individual's temperament and capabilities, is usually the most effective method of helping children achieve these goals.

It needs to be noted that if there is marital disharmony, parents will find their energies diverted and sapped by the friction and will thus be unable to give their children the attention they deserve. Also, the children will be less receptive, seeing their parents' discord, with neither side willing to forgive or compromise.

What Parents Can Do to Empower Children's Voices

As the child's first teachers, the parents' goal is to draw out the very best that potentially exists in the child. What takes place in the home is the foundation of all future learning and achievement. Under the guidance of parents, children acquire their self-images and the fundamentals of good character, which enable them to make the best use of whatever intellectual and social gifts they have.

Education in its comprehensive understanding is only partly dependent on formal living. A child who is caring and courteous is an asset to humanity, even if he is not intellectually gifted, while one who is highly educated but behaves in an antisocial manner is a menace to himself/herself and others.

Parents are expected to nurture and educate the young mind and character, a delicate, time-consuming, and complex operation. In addition to what is absorbed by the impressionable mind, parents must also be concerned with how well the mind is organized, and how it expresses itself. The responsibility of parents is to serve as loving and wise instructors, pointing out relationships, correcting faulty perceptions, and providing reassurance.

(a) Establish trust

The bedrock of emotional security is laid during an infant's earliest days, when his cries are met with loving, patient attention. If there is a consistent pattern to daily life, with no prolonged periods of hunger, discomfort, or fatigue, the baby will develop a trusting view of the world, able to rely on the fact that food and comfort come along with reassuring regularity. Moreover, unselfish parental love plays an important part in the child's growth and development, as, even if physical nourishment is provided by parents without this fundamental stability, a child will be emotionally and even physically handicapped.

As the child advances in age, he needs to know that parental love will not be withdrawn, that parents can be relied upon. If the child is aware that parents are by his side, he will also realize that they always have his best interests at heart. When they point out a flaw in his behavior, he will understand that it must be corrected because the behavior itself is wrong, not because the parents are unkind or capricious. He will not view their admonition as a rejection or condemnation of himself as a worthless person.

The process of building trust between parents and children starts early and continues through the years. It requires sincere effort from parents to see things from their child's point of view, not first their own, and to try and understand the child's own reasoning and motivation for acting in a particular way in a given situation. When parents patiently question and receive this information, they can correct faulty thinking. Children who do not have a fundamental trust in the love and concern of parents will not be able to grow up as well as those who live in assured, dependable families, nourished with a constant flow of love.

(b) Talk together

Listening intently to a child's perception and imagination can be an enchanting experience and it is exciting to watch the young mind develop as it acquires the ability to think clearly. A daily "talk time" in which the child can have his parents' undivided attention is indispensable—no career, no hobby, no demands, no household chore should interrupt this precious time of communication. All the cares of the day should be set aside to make this time "special."

Anxieties, fears, the puzzling behavior of other children, and questions about the universe and the child's place in it, can be dealt with in simple ways that are affectionate and caring. When the child is confiding something, patronizing and chastising should be replaced by being emotionally supportive and accepting. A mere shake of the head or a look sometimes helps the child realize that something went wrong—parents do not need to chastise, but can offer sympathy and encouragement, gently pointing out the way to do it right the next time. They need to reassure the child that there is always a tomorrow, there are always chances to improve.

"Talk-times" are some of the most delightful experiences of child rearing. Walking hand in hand or sitting side by side for a chat are moments that the child cherishes. Being a caring listener strengthens feelings of self-worth and gives a sense of being both cherished and valued. This will help give them the self-respect they need to treat others with respect.

(c) Bond with children

Parents always need to be patient, willing, and non-patronizing to their young children, always a friend, but also a parent. This is necessary so as not to dilute the parental role. Parents need to be parents first, friends second, and maintain the line of authority. Once the line of authority is blurred it is hard to re-establish it. This can happen, and single parents are especially susceptible. Children always need someone in charge of them, no matter how amicable that parent may be.

Being friends implies being comfortable with one another, being able to enjoy common ideas, thoughts, and activities together. Love in a family is assumed and axiomatic, but liking one another enough to seek out each other's company is the result of an accepting and warm environment. When parents themselves are fast friends, bonding with children and between siblings come more naturally.

(d) Encourage children to be independent

To encourage independence, parents need to know when to leave the child alone to explore, to find things out, and to play and interact with others. There are times when it is even wise to allow a child to make a few errors, as long as the mistakes are not life threatening or carry the risk of burning the house down!

Nearly every mistake is the result of not applying certain fundamental concepts. For example, consideration for others is a basic principle, as is kindness, safety, being careful—dozens and dozens of general principles that must be learned when growing up. Learning to behave rationally and responsibly is what maturing into independence is all about. In a sense, confident behavior is simply connecting the fundamental principles of conduct to the child's daily life.

When children make repeated mistakes, parents should take care not to angrily call attention to them but to explain the underlying logical concept behind the issue so that the mistakes are less likely to be repeated.

Starting with total dependency at birth and going on till eventual independence, the relaxation of parental control is gradual during the normal process of maturing, while the child's self-discipline and sense of inner direction grows correspondingly. In this process, responsibility is transferred to the growing child, and the goal of raising an integrated, independent person becomes achievable.

(e) Exercise discipline with love and firmness

Discipline with love and firmness recognizes the individuality of the child as a person. This becomes necessary for any family or community to function optimally. Children are inexperienced and therefore need the guidance of adults who are mature, responsible, and integrated.

The basic and fundamental tasks of the family in its relationship building must be taught early. Family is the first school of education and parents the first teachers; they enable children to become aware that there are differences between right and wrong and kindness and unkindness. With the passage of time, the child becomes conscious of the larger surroundings and family members, and realizes that there are definite privileges and responsibilities. Discipline (an unheard word these days) assists the child in his socialization process, developing his self-respect as an integral part of the whole, and helps him learn to respect the rights of others, both within the family and in the larger social community. This responsible raising of children can minimize friction and conflict in the home, and help the child develop positive socializing skills.

Discipline therefore acknowledges the rights and responsibilities of both parents and children.

(f) Affirmation—Helps build confidence and self esteem

One of the assets parents can give their children is to help them develop a deep reservoir of self-esteem that will not only allow them to fulfil their potential, but will also carry them through the inevitable stresses of life.

Young people who have the assurance of self-esteem and self-reliance believe they have some control over their destinies and do have a voice. Unafraid to undertake new ventures, they feel quite optimistic and easily attract the friendship of others. They feel that as long as they make an effort, they can achieve stability in life. Other children who have the same natural intelligence but low self-esteem are less competent, unwilling to volunteer, abandon tasks at the first signs of difficulty, have few social skills to maintain friendships and frequently say "I can't" or "I am not able to." (Paul Chance. (1986). Your Child's Self-Esteem).

The question is: How can we raise children who will have a voice and adults who will encourage children to express that voice?

There is no specific recipe—only the assurance that if children are enabled to develop healthy attitudes they begin to develop a positive self-image and self-confidence. Positive action takes many forms. Although not every child will receive top grades in academic subjects in school, he or she can still be made to feel successful. Talent is abundant, but children need to be given space, opportunity, and appreciation to express that talent and to have a say in what pertains to his or her life and future.

(g) Identifying with children: Seeing through their eyes and using language they can understand

The fragile and tender voices and nature of children call for protection. Their hearts are delicate, their feelings sensitive, and, although we may not be aware of it, their views on matters that affect them are perceptive.

The life of a child can be compared to a flower, the sensitivity of their feelings to clean water, while the acuteness of their vision reminds us of a strong microscope: the first will wither and fade away at the first sign of rough handling, the second will be clouded and polluted by the least amount of agitation, while the third will make them keen sighted and precise. (Ali-Akbar Firutan (1980) Mothers, Fathers and Children; Practical Advice to Parents). When we try to look at the world through the eyes of our children, we will become attuned to them, and instead of seeing things from our adult perspective, we will be able to work with them from their perceptions and points of view.

Through these experiences they will learn empathy—the ability to share in the emotional states of others. They will learn two essential components of positive socialization—to be considerate and to have no wish to harm others. They will learn to control their negative feelings, refrain from being overly critical, and practice forbearance. As parents, we can help children control themselves.

Parental Behavior

Emotional well-being

Family and home are not just places where a group of people meet or live; they have an ambience and spirit of their own, where certain conditions must be present to create a general sense of well-being and emotional bonding.

(a) *Truthfulness*

Truthfulness is the base on which lasting and successful relationships are built. Lack of honesty and truthfulness corrode relationships and children should not be prevented from "saying it as it is." They should also be listened to carefully. Silencing a child leads to dominance and fear and eventually he becomes entrapped in a web of lies, to the extent that it becomes a dominant feature of his character. Speaking the truth is giving a voice to the child, to speak and be heard.

(b) *Consistency*

It represents a fundamental harmony and integrity in conduct. It is a stepping stone to burning away the fog of confusion and uncertainty. It brings stability, defines boundaries, establishes expectations, and provides for the orderly dispensing of rewards.

(c) *Flexibility*

Flexibility is certainly not an uncompromising rigidity in family and/or social relationships. One can be inconsistent yet rigid. Rigidity implies taking a position irrespective of merits. Sometimes a child may be refused a reasonable request without thinking it through. Then the child refuses to relent even when a legitimate request is made of him.

When a very young child says something untrue, the most appropriate response may simply be to rephrase the whole story into the truth instead of scolding the child. Flexibility in thought and action calls for sensitivity, especially to young children who often have difficulty in distinguishing fantasy from fact.

(d) *Reverence*

Reverence is a mixture of love, respect, and courtesy. It should be shown to oneself, others, the whole of creation, and the Creator. Reverence is the cornerstone on which appreciative attitudes are built, and children need to develop this attitude at the earliest possible age.

Reverence is found in the value of human life. Any form of disregard or harm to human life manifests itself in antisocial behavior and goes hand in hand with contempt for human life.

(e) ***Apologizing***

The fear of losing authority often does not allow parents to apologize when they make a mistake. This is unwise for several reasons. (Joyce and Vedral. 'I'm Sorry,' Parents Magazine 62)

When children hear their parents express regret, they learn to say sorry too. Knowing that parents also can make mistakes teaches children to be more self-accepting. If a child never hears apologies, he may think that apologizing is a sign of weakness. Parents can maintain their dignity and also show that being wrong is not shameful—a sincere apology is an honorable way to admit mistakes. When a parent says "I am sorry I hurt your feelings," it shows that parents really care about how the child feels. Apologies should be made after anger has subsided and one is sincerely sorry. It then clears the air of troubled feelings and the incident can be laid to rest.

(f) ***Laughter and humor***

A home without laughter is like a garden without flowers. We are all capable of enjoying this priceless gift of life and giving joy to others. A sense of humor needs to be developed. The best kind of humor is that which does not involve having fun at someone else's expense. Family humor should be free of racial, ethnic, and gender bias as well as abusive language. An Eastern saying goes: "Teasing and mockery are sharp scissors that can sever any relationship." We should make sure that humor permeates family life so that the children join in and automatically acquire the love of laughter.

Growing in a Larger World and Exercising One's Voice

As children grow toward adulthood, their attention turns to the larger world. They are interested in issues that relate to life beyond the intimacy of the family home: planning for a career, raising unprejudiced children, and so on. This century sees the outline of the dynamic societies in which our children will spend most of their lives. We have to prepare them to be competent and confident in the years that lie ahead despite the rapidity of change and the onslaught of technology.

The way family members treat each other has a great influence on whether the children will grow up believing in the equality of men and women. Does the father listen to the mother with respect? Are the major decisions of the family made jointly? Does the mother refuse to be spoken to rudely by anyone in the family? Are the daughters challenged intellectually and encouraged to plan their careers with the same seriousness as the sons? If sons are not trained to believe in the equality of men and women, they may have a difficult time with women in authority at work, as well as a problem finding and keeping a wife who will be happy in a subservient role. If daughters are not made to feel equally capable of achieving to the best of their abilities, they may remain arrested in their development, and the larger world will be deprived of their unique contributions.

The Role of the State in Supporting Healthy Marriages, Strengthening the Two-Parent Family and Protecting Children

"Family" is pivotal to the past, present, and future of humanity. Family affects and is affected by trends, changes, and transformations. The International Year of the Family (IYF) Occasional Paper says: "The relative strength of a nation or society depends largely on the strength of its families. What occurs in families affects the whole of society, and vice versa. There is a complicated relationship between the two." The article titled Future of Children" (Woodrow Wilson School of Public and International Affairs at Princeton University and The Brooklyn Institute Vol. 15, No 2) has this to say: "It would be a mistake for policy makers to focus on marriage to the exclusion of other strategies. Among such strategies, alleviating poverty, improving parent–child bonds and reducing teenage childbearing and unintended pregnancies are especially promising. Efforts to reduce out-of-wedlock births, teenage pregnancy in particular, are an essential part of a marriage and should not be a proxy for cutting programs for single parents. Programs to encourage fathers' involvement – both monetary and emotional – must be continued. A strong child support system and a fair court system that encourages joint involvement of separating parents must be continued and improved. All these programs are crucial to the overall mission to increase the number of healthy marriages and improve the overall wellbeing of children."

This background brings us to a crucial question: While families exist apart from the State, do "Families" have a role in supporting the Family? With the experience of three decades of working with families in over 45 countries and as the author of this article, I believe the reply is an uncompromising "Yes." No Nation State can abdicate its responsibilities, ignore or transfer to any other institution the duty of providing for the safety of the family and well-being of its members by being proactive both in supporting the health of intact marriages and in supporting families which are at risk and need assistance. A US document states: "The State can only recognize and acknowledge these rights. In the same manner, the family is a gift that the State should not deny or manipulate for its own purposes. The State must recognize and respect the family for what it is, as a matter of fundamental and moral law. By intruding on the prerogatives of the family or ignoring the decline of the family, the State weakens its very foundation. The State's foremost obligation in this sphere is to respect, defend and protect the family as an institution." (Developed by the Administration for Children and Families, US Department of Health and Human Services).

It is a fundamental need to ensure a positive and loving family environment and thereby prevent many social ills that are increasingly erupting in almost all countries and which place individuals, families, nations, and our very world at risk. The State must recognize the unique and irreplaceable contribution of both mothers and fathers to the well-being of their children and the contribution a united family makes to the community and nation.

The State ought to do what it can to introduce and strengthen healthy marriages by including positive and healthy sexuality education programs in all educational institutions, launching pre-marriage guidance programs to prepare persons of marriageable age to know and understand the responsibilities of parenthood, and setting up therapy and counseling cells in public, private, and health settings for couples who are embroiled in difficulties. In doing so the State does not remain neutral but becomes an active participant, creating conditions that allow family stability, longevity, and autonomy to become active and thrive.

The State ought to strive to keep tax burdens and prices of food and essential commodities as low as possible so that families are not overburdened by taxes and, instead, have the purchasing power to provide adequate food nutrition and basic facilities to all members, especially children.

The State must realize and respect the dignity and worth of every person and child regardless of state of birth (out of wedlock, teenage pregnancy, etc.) and family structure or status. All human beings and every child are unique gifts to humanity and to families, and deserve protection, care, nurture, and safety at home, institutions, and in society. It is against this overarching backdrop that all policies of the State should support the Family and enable it to exercise its "transforming role."

Conclusion

Nation States have a choice—they can support on an urgent basis pro-family policies and/or family-friendly facilities and experience its incredible benefits to their national story and the stories of children, adults, families and societies throughout the world; or they can contribute to family, community, national, global chaos, disaster, and ultimately suicide by legalizing anti-family, anti-conception, and anti-birth policies and programs. All crucial decisions that affect families and the future of humanity depend on the integrity, moral caliber, and social conscience of contemporary elected leadership, including the United Nations. The challenge before an effective leadership is to take to heart the youth of today and guide the future of humanity in constructive directions to create a new and just world order based on truth, love, and justice. This new world order must seek to place "Family" at the heart of public policy and global dialogue, and enable future generations to reap the best possible harvest. Denying "Family" its rightful place by compromising the legal framework to suit, adopt, and support popular notions based on selfishness and self-centeredness is to manipulate the nature of the twin institutions of Marriage and Family, undermine the foundation and cornerstone of society, and in the process, deprive children of their rightful voice and deprive the Family of its power to transform society.

References

UN IYF Occasional Papers Series 1992 No 2, *Family: Forms and Functions,* Chapter 2, *Basic care of children and relatives* p. 9

Beam Joe: Marriage Helper 911 article: *Trickle Down Parenting: Your Marriage and Parenting*
http://www.marriagehelper.com/marriageandchildren.php

Khavari, Khalil A & Khavari, Sue Williamson, *Creating a Successful Family*, p 11, Sterling Publishers Pvt. Ltd, New Delhi 1100010

Lazlo, Ervin *et al* (1948) *Goals for Mankind - A Report to the Club of Rome on the New Horizon of Global Community* p. iii. Rev. Edu. New York: New American Library

Ewy, Donna & Ewy, Rodger, 1985: *Preparation for Parenthood: How to Create a Nurturing Family - Part I,* New York, New American Library

Chance, Paul: *Your Child's Self Esteem, Annual Editions of Psychology,* 86/87, Guilford, Conn. Dushkin 1986 p.153-158

Firutan, Ali-Akbar, 1980: *Mothers, Fathers and Children Practical Advice to Parents*, Oxford, George Ronald p. 26

Vedral, Joyce. L: *I'm Sorry* Parents Magazine No 62, April 1987, p. 91-94

UN IYF Occasional Papers Series No. 2, 1992. *Family Forms and Functions, Introduction - Towards a Conceptualisation of Family*, p.1

Woodrow Wilson School of Public and International Affairs at Princeton University and The Brooklyn Institute: *The Future of our Children* Vol. 15, No 2 Fall 2005. Marriage is Part of a Broader Goal of Reducing Poverty and Increasing Child Wellbeing

Department of Health and Human Services: *A Celebration of Family - Observance of the Tenth Anniversary of the International Year of the Family* October 2004, No 7, p. 3

CHAPTER TWO

ALL CHILDREN ARE OUR CHILDREN, WHY THE NEGLECT?

H. B. DANESH*

The theme *Giving Children a Voice: The Transforming Role of the Family in a Global Society* covers issues pertaining to the condition of the world's children, conditions both positive and negative, tragic and promising, difficult and hopeful, including the tragic reality that many children are cheated of their childhood. Giving children a voice refers to a worldwide movement gaining increasing momentum and ever-higher prominence on the agenda of humanity. The voice of children is most effectively heard through their bewildered, sorrowful, and questioning response to the ways that adults treat them. The look of a hungry child, a sick child, a child living in a slum, in a war zone, in an inner city ghetto, in a loveless luxurious residence, in a sterile and controlling environment – these looks have their own silent voice and tell many tales of neglect, abuse, cruelty, and indifference committed by adults and institutions of society.

We live in a world in which around 51 million births go unregistered every year; approximately 158 million children aged 5–14 are engaged in child labor; an estimated 1.2 million children are trafficked every year; and at any given time, over 300,000 child soldiers, some as young as eight, are exploited in armed conflict; more than one million children worldwide are detained by law enforcement officials; approximately two million children are exploited through prostitution and pornography; tens of millions of girls below age 18 are forced into marriage; and a similar

---

* This chapter is partially based on two chapters of a new book "*Unity of Faith and Reason in Action: A Journey of Discovery*" by the author, published by Juxta Publishing in 2010. Full approval of Juxta Publishing is obtained for the references made in this chapter drawn from this book.

number of young women and girls are subjected to genital mutilation. (UNICEF, 2008) We, collective adults, have created a world of conflict, corruption, violence, prejudice, poverty, and injustice that makes our children its direct victims, gives them appalling role models, and leaves them a terrible world as their inheritance.

Children survive and thrive in the context of relationships within their families, communities, and societies. Each of these entities has specific, but interrelated, responsibilities for providing healthy environments for the wholesome development of children with regard to their physical, emotional, intellectual, social, and spiritual needs. Neglect of any of these areas of need greatly affects the life of the child and the nature of his or her relationships with self, others and the world. It is in the context of relationships that children are educated and learn about themselves and the world and about life and its joys and sorrows. Thus, the quality of the life of our children is the yardstick by which we can measure the quality of our parenting practices, the nature of our relationship with children, and the standard of our leadership. This close association between the nature of our parenting, relationship, and leadership with children and the condition of their lives poses several questions.

Question One: Who is responsible for the care of children?
Parents Only? Parents and the Government? All of us?

Question Two: What is the most significant predictor of children's future?
Their economic conditions? Safety of their environments? The type of parenting and education they receive? All of them?

Question Three: Why do we tolerate such a degree of cruelty and neglect of children? Is it because we do not care? Because they are not our children? Because these children deserve it? Why?

Let us consider each of these questions separately.

Who is responsible for the care of children? Clearly, parents have the primary responsibility for all aspects of the lives of their children. However, because the lives of parents are greatly affected by the nature of communities in which they live and by the types of governance they experience, it follows that society also has specific responsibilities for the care of children. Among these are the responsibilities to create violence-free, safe, and peaceful communities and schools; to provide reasonable health and medical care; to address the needs of the poor and the less-privileged members of society; and to ensure the protection of human rights of all members of society with specific attention to the rights of children and youth.

The second question—*What is the most significant predictor of children's future?*—encompasses many factors, including the issues of poverty, healthcare, safety, quality of parenting, and type of education that children receive. There is ample empirical and research evidence that these and other related factors dramatically affect children's lives. The common factor in all these situations is the quality of relationships and education that children receive. Good relationships build resilient, optimistic, motivated, and unifying personalities; and good education nurtures and develops intellectual capacities, creative potential, and spiritual aspirations. Children thus trained are often able to remove themselves from the adverse environments into which they are born.

The third question—*Why do we tolerate such a degree of cruelty and neglect of children?*—is the most challenging. There are many reasons for this terrible fact. Many parents and leaders unfortunately do not care about the condition of the world's children. Others primarily care about their own children. And still others, one hopes a very small number, blame underprivileged children for their own miseries. These are troubling assertions and we can dismiss them as too pessimistic and even inaccurate. But the fact remains that millions of children live in the most appalling of circumstances. Many are hungry, sick, and neglected. Many die of preventable diseases. Many have no shelter, are deprived of the most basic care and live truly miserable lives. And all these are happening in a world that is much richer, knowledgeable, connected, and capable than ever it has been in the history of humanity.

We and other privileged members of the world community must face these realities and must ask why so many children suffer so greatly. And we need to ask ourselves, "What are our individual and collective responsibilities toward the world's neglected children?" and "What can we do to remedy the situation?"

Searching for New Solutions

In our search for new solutions, we first need to identify the nature and the underlying causes of the neglect of children. On the basis of the insights drawn from many research reports and empirical data, as well as on my five decades of work with children, families, schools and other institutions of society, I put forward the following six propositions for consideration:

> **Proposition One:** The two main culprits for the appalling condition of the world's children are violence and poverty that together have created a culture of poverty (Harrington 1962, Lewis 1975 & 1979, Moynihan 1965, Rosenberg) and a culture of violence (Baker 1993; Danesh 2008a,b,c; UNESCO 2008), which are present, in one form or another, in practically all countries and territories of the world.
> **Proposition Two:** Poverty and violence are totally interrelated and together contribute to the weakening of the central institutions of society—family, government, and civil society.
> **Proposition Three:** The weakening of the institutions of society in turn gives birth to some of the most glaring examples of human violence, such as hunger, disease, abuse, and neglect, which afflict countless children and their parents around the globe.
> **Proposition Four:** Human violence is primarily fuelled by conflict-based mindsets and worldviews that provide the framework within which we interpret reality, understand human nature, ascertain the purpose of life, and justify our actions and our relationships.
> **Proposition Five:** Our worldviews are formed on the basis of our unique life experiences and the lessons we learn at home, in the school, and in the community through both formal and informal education.
> **Proposition Six:** The primary requisite for transforming the existing cultures of violence and poverty to those of peace and prosperity is a universal program of peace-based education in the context of a just economic system that ensures fulfilment of the essential human needs and rights for survival (food, shelter, health, education, work,and security); association (equality, freedom, justice, and rule of law); and supraordinate human needs (need for meaning, purpose, and freedom of conscience) for everyone. (Danesh, 2011)

On the basis of these six propositions, it is evident that the current worldwide crises with regard to the care of the world's children require both *urgent short-term* and *deliberate long-term* programs. Short-term programs need to simultaneously stop all types of violence and alleviate crushing poverty, along with their terrible offspring: hunger, disease, homelessness, hopelessness, and so on. Deliberate long-term approach refers to a fundamental transformation in the education of our children and youth, preparing them to be active and contributing members of their respective societies with the aim of creating a global civilization of peace.

Currently, many individuals, institutions, and governments, with varying degrees of success, are addressing the short-term challenges, but few are focused on the long-term strategies. However, short-term efforts alone will not remedy the situation. There is ample evidence that despite many short-term programs, the condition of the world's children continues to be dire and is threatening to overwhelm those individuals, institutions, and governments that are engaged in emergency assistance to children. The sheer extent of problems that are increasing at an alarming rate in all parts of the world indicates that we need to simultaneously focus on both the short-term and long-term strategies required for the betterment of the state of the world's children.

In this chapter, I address one of the most essential components of the long-term strategy required for the betterment of the condition of children—education for creating a culture of peace. In doing so, I draw from my decades of experience, research, and study as a physician, psychiatrist, family therapist, and, more recently, as a peace educator. I have had the opportunity to live in three continents of the world—Asia (the Middle East), North America (Canada and the United States), and Europe (Switzerland)—and to travel to over seventy countries on all continents. During these travels I have observed with concern the alarming signs of deterioration in the conditions of children and youth in both rich and poor countries from Bosnia to Brazil, Japan to Jamaica, Canada to China, Iceland to India, Malawi to Malaysia, Switzerland to South Africa, Russia to Romania, and the United States to the United Kingdom.

I will elaborate on an integrated approach to the education of children and their parents and caregivers, with a focus on the psychological, social, and spiritual needs of children. I will not address the issues of poverty, hunger, disease, and violence, not because I consider them unimportant—they are indeed extremely important—but rather because I believe these tragic situations are the results of certain fundamental flaws in our approach to families and children. In a world where children die by the thousands every day, are used as soldiers, are trained to be suicide bombers, and commit suicide at an ever younger age, the problems we are facing are more profound and deep-rooted. There is both financial poverty and poverty of spirit. There is hunger for food and hunger for righteousness, love, and compassion. There is physical disease and the disease of the soul. We need to transcend the barriers of political talk, diplomatic discourse, correct speech, and ideological assertions, barriers that prevent us from speaking clearly, openly, and frankly about what has gone wrong in our ways of thinking and behaving that has allowed for such a tragic disaster with our children and youth.

Distinguished educator, John Dewey (1859–1952) observed that education is a process of living and not preparation for future living" (1897, p. 1)This implies that we never stop learning and with regard to the manner in which the adults of the world are caring for the children of the world, there is clearly much for us to learn. Therefore, the focus on education here has two objectives. The first objective is for us as adults, parents, caregivers, educators, policymakers, leaders, health professionals, and scholars to reflect on the kind of education that is conducive to prevention of child neglect and abuse in our world. This process will have both learning and transformative outcomes. Ultimately, we need to transform adults' approach to children in order to transform the condition of the world's children. The second objective is for us to rear and educate all children in a way that those who are now in danger of falling victims to neglect and abuse will be protected; and that all children would be helped to grow to become the type of adults who are able and willing to take care of the coming generations of children with greater sensitivity and insight than is the case now. This is an essential task, because as Pope John Paul II observed; "As the family goes, so goes the nation and so goes the whole world in which we live."

I will primarily focus on three areas of education—educating for self-knowledge, educating the family, and educating for peace—which I believe are among the main requisites for improving the condition of children everywhere. Educational needs of children are directly related to the cardinal responsibilities of the family, community, and society. This shared responsibility is due to the fact that in the final analysis *all* children are *our* children. Humanity is one and nowhere is our fundamental oneness more convincingly felt than by the manner in which we as individuals and groups respond to children and the ease and trust with which children accept appropriate parenting from adults.

Educating for Self-Knowledge

Achieving true freedom

In its broadest and most inclusive application, there are three kinds of education: material, human, and spiritual. *Material education* refers to the physical development, nutrition, health, and comfort of the body. *Human education* refers to psychological and social education of the children. It is concerned, at once, with the mental and emotional development of the child and the progress of society and the development of civilization, encompassing such issues as government, administration, charitable works, science, arts, technology, and all other such activities as we observe in human societies in various stages of progress and refinement. *Spiritual education* is concerned with the development of virtues, high standards of morality, and living life according to the ethical principles of truth and truthfulness, unity building in the context of diversity and dedication to the cause of compassion, service, justice, and peace. (Abdu'l-Bahá, 1987).

Parents and educators need to help their children to develop an understanding of themselves as unique individuals possessing enormous intellectual, artistic, emotional, and spiritual potential that can be conducive to their glory, honour, and greatness. The secret here lies in the human capacity for self-knowledge, which is only possible in the context of an integrated and comprehensive education. Self-knowledge has at least three dimensions: physical, psychosocial, and spiritual. In our world, today, we are most knowledgeable about the physical dimension of ourselves. Modern science has made enormous strides in this regard. We now know much more about physical and biological aspects of our being and are fascinated by our on-going discoveries. This knowledge, although incomplete and continually changing, has become the source of fascination for many scientists and has even convinced many scientists that we humans are basically physical/biological beings and that the psychological and spiritual dimensions of our humanness originate from our physical reality. The human individual is an integrated unity of "body and mind" and of "material and spiritual." Self-knowledge requires an understanding of all aspects of being human—physical, mental, emotional, and spiritual—that operates in a state of unity and integration in life. Education, therefore, needs to introduce children to the dynamics and qualities of the law of unity that is operative at all levels of existence and life. Unity is, at once, a scientific and spiritual state and its understanding is essential for *life-knowledge*, in general and *self-knowledge*, in particular. The task of starting children on the path of self-knowledge—a process that has a beginning and no end—requires that parents, schools, and communities, together be mindful of its requirements. In this task, the insights gained from both science and religion are essential and must be offered to children in a manner that will ensure that as they grow up and continue on the path of their maturation, they will grow to be physically healthy, psychologically mature, socially unifying, economically productive, and spiritually enlightened and universal.

This integrated approach to education calls for a fundamental rethinking of the current practices of the training and instruction of children at home, in the schools, and within the community. At the core of this rethinking is the issue of the type of education necessary for transcending human selfishness, which is considered by some to be a "natural" aspect of human nature. (Gould, 1990, Dawkins 2006, Sterelny 2007, Wilson & Wilson 2007) At the biological level we are, by necessity, selfish. Like all other living entities, humans are biologically programmed for self-preservation, pain-avoidance, and pleasure seeking. The powerful pull of these proclivities inclines human beings to be mainly concerned with their own safety and satisfaction. However, when this proclivity takes place in the context of exclusion or conditional inclusion of others, then human relationships suffer profoundly. Relationships are essential for a healthy and productive life and in the context of selfishness they are weakened and often disrupted.

A wholesome and integrated education, with its focus on the biological, intellectual, emotional, social, moral, and spiritual development of the individual in the context of the consciousness of the oneness of humanity, is acutely needed. It is essential for helping us and our children to be increasingly less selfish and more other-oriented and universal in our relationships. It is in this context that unalloyed love takes root and brings forth fruits of mercy, compassion, equality, justice, unity, and peace, which are so badly needed in our world.

Educatingthe Family—Equality at Last

Children and Parenting

Our approach to parenting is a reflection of the nature of our self-knowledge and knowledge of others. Whenever and wherever there are children, there automatically comes into being a "family." The very presence of children puts adults and the environment surrounding them, in the role of the family. However, when the family is not based on solid ground and committed sentiments and resolves, it will not be able to parent adequately. Children by nature need protection, nurturing, care, guidance, and encouragement, which are the main properties of parental love. Children also need adult role models to emulate in order to adequately prepare themselves to become contributing adults in society. To the degree that these fundamental needs of children are met, to that same degree children grow up to be protective, nurturing, caring, enlightened, and encouraging adults and capable, healthy parents. In other words, children reared in healthy, loving families usually grow up to be healthy and loving adults, capable of creating marriages and families characterized by unity, equality, and creativity. These are among the essential characteristics of the "unity-based family," which I have described elsewhere. (Danesh, 1995)

As we contemplate the condition of the majority of the world's children, one fact becomes obvious: our children are not being adequately and properly parented. In the war-ravaged regions of the world, children are the most tragic victims. In poverty-stricken areas, children suffer the most. Where adequate hygiene and medical care are lacking, children die in the greatest numbers. In affluent societies, children are relegated to a tertiary level of priority after the economic, professional, and personal interests and pursuits of their parents. Wherever people face racism and prejudice, children are the most innocent and helpless victims. There is hardly anywhere in the world where we can say with confidence that the majority of children are being reared under adequately healthy, caring, and loving conditions conducive to their wholesome development, even at a moderate level. This is so because the institution of the family has become feeble and is often unable to meet the requirements and demands of change in the contemporary world. Neither oppressive and authoritarian traditional families, nor chaotic conflicted modern families engaged in their internal power struggle, are suitable to the needs of this new phase in the evolution of humanity. A new type of family and a new approach to the all-important task of rearing our children is needed.

The family, as the workshop of civilization, is an indispensable part of civilized life. As such, we cannot be without it. However, the kind of family that the world now needs is not the kind we generally find in our world. A dramatically different type of family is needed, which I have designated as the unity-based family.

Characteristics of Unity-Based Families

The unity-based family refers to the type of family in which gender equality is not only a right but also a responsibility of all members of the family. However, because of the inequality that now exists between men and women with respect to their education, wealth, power and leadership opportunities within the family and in society, women and girls must be given at least equal, preferably priority, rights and opportunities until equitable and equal conditions are attained. For far too long, humanity has been deprived of women's unique contributions at an optimal level toward the development of civilization. The very quality of our world will change for the better when women are involved on an equal basis with men, in the administration of all human affairs—political, academic, religious, economic, and so on—and are given the opportunity to make their unique contributions to the life of both the family and society under equal, just, and enlightened conditions. That is why the education of women must top the agenda of all nations, governments, and social agencies of the world.

Equality is a sign of maturity and maturity is the process of an ever-increasing ability to integrate and unite rather than to differentiate and separate. Excessive and self-centred individualism is the hallmark of the adolescent phase of growth. It is a condition of self-absorption and self-worship. It does not include others except for one's own benefit. Equality, conversely, is a state of unity and integration. It is a relationship characterized by willingness and ability to be cooperative, generous, and other-directed. In the contemporary world, when humanity is traversing its most problematic phase of collective adolescence, the quest for equality between women and men often deteriorates into a virulent and destructive power struggle. The very instruments—power, force, and competition—by which men have always achieved their self-centred interests are now being sought by women in order to correct the injustices of the past and present; hence, the potentially destructive power struggle present in many marriages and families. This is not surprising because power struggle is the most common outcome of the power-based human relationships which are highly prevalent during this crucial phase of humanity's collective coming of age. At the beginning of the 20th century, the following observation was made by one of the most outstanding religious figures of our time—'Abdu'l-Bahá:

> The world in the past has been ruled by force and man has dominated over woman by reason of his more forceful and aggressive qualities both of body and mind. But the balance is already shifting; force is losing its dominance and mental alertness, intuition and the spiritual qualities of love and service, in which woman is strong, are gaining ascendancy. Hence the new age will be an ageless masculine and more permeated with the feminine ideals, or, to speak more exactly, will be an age in which the masculine and feminine elements of civilization will be more evenly balanced. (1987, p. 149)

Educating for Peace

From Oppression to Unity in Diversity

The third pillar of a long-term program for correcting the condition of the world's children is the vital and indispensable task of educating every new generation of children and youth according to the universal principles of peace:

- Humanity is one.
- The oneness of humanity is expressed in diversity.
- The twin crucial challenges before humanity always are to safeguard our oneness and to nurture our diversity.
- The true expression of our humanness is to achieve these two tasks according to the principle of unity in diversity, without recourse to violence.

In my considered view, when a society begins to educate every new generation of its children and youth in their homes, schools, and communities, according to the principles of peace, then such a society, in a span of a few decades, will begin to experience a most dramatic positive transformation in all areas of its individual and collective life, including the welfare of its children. This assertion needs further elaboration.

The Folly of Conflict-BasedEducation

The lamentable condition of millions of children and youth in our world clearly indicates that many societies, for whatever reason, are not fulfilling their fundamental responsibilities as the ultimate guardians of the children in their populations. Among the most consequential neglect of children is with respect to the type of education they receive. There is a crisis in the intellectual, emotional, social, moral, and spiritual education of children. One common aspect of this crisis concerns the issue of peace-based education, the lack of which causes much misery in all societies.

We not only fail to offer systematic peace-based education to our children and youth, we rather tend to educate our children within the framework of conflict. In their families and communities, the majority of the world's children receive religious, ethnic, class, and cultural indoctrination and education, usually in the context of ideas and practices based on in-group and out-group, us and them, citizens and foreigners, civilized and barbaric, rich and poor, good and bad, and the saved and the damned perspectives. In schools, the history taught to our children is often the history of conflict. The geography learned is often the geography of conflict. The literature studied is literature infused with conflict. The biology or economics or political science our children learn is frequently taught within the framework of conflict. We give our children a conflict-based education. Hence the alarming prevalence of conflict, violence, and hostility in our world!

In my view, the conditions of the world will not improve unless we adopt a peace-based curriculum of instruction for all children and youth and, for that matter, for all parents, teachers, and community and political leaders. This aspect of education is gravely overlooked at home, in schools, in communities, and in the media, which has emerged as one of the most influential sources of education of our children and youth. Families need guidance and assistance on how to rear their children as peaceful and peace-creating individuals, and this task needs to be shared by parents and schools, governments and policymakers, social, academic and religious institutions, as well as by media and health professionals dealing with the family.

Requisites of peace

The fundamental requisites of peace are truthfulness (transparency), equality, justice, and unity. These requisites are hallmarks of maturity born out of personal responsibility in the context of self-knowledge and societal responsibility based on the consciousness of the oneness of humanity. We are hard pressed to find, anywhere, significant examples of the integrated presence of these interdependent fundamental requisites for human well-being and development, either in families or societies. Usually, one or more of these requisites are missing.

These interdependent requisites have the quality of hologram—each part contains the whole. In other words, in order to achieve all of these conditions, we need to begin with at least one of them. Thus, for example, when we attempt to create equality in a family, the other four conditions—truthfulness, justice, unity, and peace—also begin to happen. This is so because it is impossible to have any of these conditions without the presence of the other requisites. The establishment of these conditions of human well-being and progress is developmental in nature. The more evolved—in psychological, social, ethical, and spiritual terms—an individual, institution, or society is, the more it is capable of establishing equality, justice, unity, and peace in the context of maturity—responsibility, freedom, and transparency. Maturity, here, refers to the development of human consciousness with its biological, psychological, social, moral, and spiritual expressions. The diagram below (Fig.1) depicts the integrated nature of the qualities and requisites of peace.

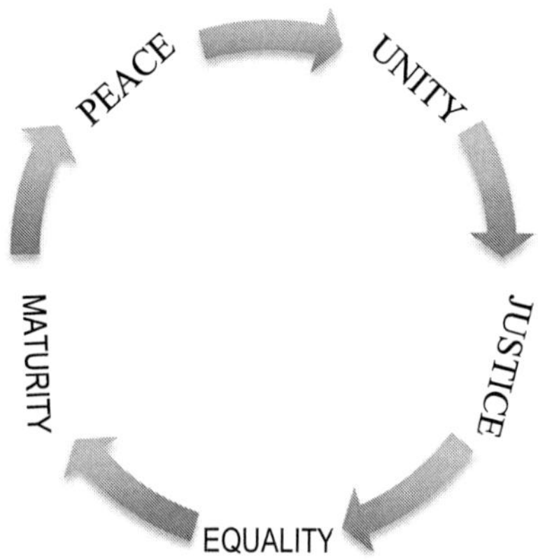

Fig. 1: Requisites of Peace

Of these conditions, unity is most accessible in terms of its quality and outward expression in human relationships. In other words, it is much easier to know when unity, rather than equality, justice, maturity, or peace, is present. These other conditions are more subjective and vague than unity. With respect to the family, the focus on unity automatically requires the presence of principles of equality, justice, and truthfulness in family relationships, simply because it is impossible to have a united and peaceful family in the absence of equality, justice, and truthfulness and responsible discharge of our responsibilities as spouses, parents, and children. Family peace is the natural outcome of these conditions and is an essential condition for a stable and peaceful society.

The primary task before parents, educators, and others who are concerned with the welfare of children is to ensure that the principles of peace and the practice of unity in diversity, are fully understood, universally promoted, and systematically implemented at all levels and within all institutions of the society—family, school, work-place, government, and religion.

This discourse on parenting and education demonstrates the enormity of the task before us as parents, citizens, and leaders in our evermore integrated world. It, therefore, behoves us to consider the task of parenting as an integral aspect of the type of formal and informal education we receive, the profession and occupation we choose, the life-priorities we set for ourselves and the deliberate efforts we make to help to provide a peace-based education for all children—ours and others.

Creating a Civilization of Peace

It is helpful to briefly discuss the requisites of a *civilization of peace*, which until now has eluded humanity throughout its history. Creation of a civilization of peace—united and diverse, equal and just, prosperous and benevolent, scientifically progressive and spiritually enlightened, technologically advanced and environmentally healthy—is the next fundamental challenge of humankind, a challenge which may require a few centuries to be optimally fulfilled. Such an accomplishment is the acme of all human accomplishments and will dramatically change the nature and quality of human life on this planet. Among the main characteristics of a civilization of peace are the absence of the current cultures of violence and poverty and the prevalence of conditions of peace and prosperity in their stead.

Practical examples of how we may be able to effectively and on a large scale tackle the issues of violence and poverty, thus paving the way for creating a civilization of peace, are hard to identify. I will briefly focus on two successful programs—Education for Peace in Bosnia and Herzegovina and the Oportunidades Project in Mexico. As I am directly involved and therefore more familiar with the Education for Peace (EFP) Program, I will describe it more fully.

The Promise of Education for Peace

The greatest challenges before humanity at the start of the 21st century are conflict, violence, terrorism, and war along with their terrible consequences of poverty, hunger, disease, despair, environmental destruction, and poor leadership. These challenges are felt at all levels of human life—the family, school, community, society, and globally. While considerable resources have always been and still are spent to offset the costly ravages of conflict, violence and war, and to pay for the high price of military defence and security measures, there are very few programs dedicated to a systematic, sustained plan of action to educate children and youth in the principles of peace. Consequently, every new generation repeats the mistakes of former generations and conflict and violence become permanent facets of human societies. Paradoxically, our greatest opportunity at this time in history is the fact that we have sufficient resources to create a civilization of peace. Peace-based education is the most essential tool for achieving this historic undertaking.

Conceptual Framework

Peace and education are inseparable aspects of civilization. No civilization is truly progressive without education and no education system is truly civilizing unless it is based on the universal principles of peace. However, our homes, schools, and communities have become increasingly conflicted and violent. We, therefore, inadvertently promote a culture of conflict and violence, and, consequently, our children do not learn the ways of peace. To adequately respond to these monumental challenges and opportunities, we need to lay the foundations of a sustainable and universal civilization of peace by better understanding the nature and dynamics of peace at all levels of human experience—intrapersonal, interpersonal, intergroup, international, and global. For this purpose, at least three synergistic and essential tasks must be pursued locally, nationally, and globally:

a. **Peace-based Education:** To educate every new generation of the world's children and youth—with the help of their parents/guardians and teachers—to become peacemakers,
b. **Peace-based Governance:** To create forums for the leaders of the world at local, regional, national, international, and global levels to study and implement the principles of peace-based governance in their respective communities and institutions.
c. **Peace-based Conflict Resolution:** To offer training opportunities in the principles and skills of conflict prevention and peace-based conflict resolution for citizens and leaders at local, regional, national, international, and global levels. (Danesh, 2011a)

The programs of the International Education for Peace Institute and its sister entities are designed to specifically address these three fundamental requisites of a civilization of peace.

The EFP Program was introduced in three primary and three secondary schools in Bosnia and Herzegovina in May 2000, five years after a most calamitous interethnic war among the Bosniak (primarily Muslim), Croat (primarily Catholic), and Serb (primarily Eastern Orthodox) populations of this small country. The pilot project involved 6,000 students, 400 teachers, and school staff and thousands of parents/guardians.

During the EFP pilot phase (2000–2002) and to some degree in 2009 (and even now in 2014), questions remain about the long-term future of Bosnia and Herzegovina. Extreme nationalism, interethnic tensions, and simmering discontent and suspicion were very high at the start of 21st millennium. The economic situation was desperate; corruption was widespread; and the relative extremes of wealth and poverty, resulting from unscrupulous economic practices during the war years, added to the people's discontent and mistrust. Feelings of maltreatment and injustice were particularly high among the citizens, and the state institutions were too weak and ineffectual to address these manifold challenges.

Added to these daily life challenges were the unattended scars of the war on children and adults alike, a condition that was being increasingly expressed in severe psychological, social, and medical disorders such as depression, addiction, delinquency, suicide, aggression, apathy, and a host of other symptoms, all indicative of a state of *resigned uncertainty, hopelessness, and confusion* with regard to their past, present, and future. No effective, broadly available, healing process from the traumatic experiences of the war and the on-going unabated conflict was evident and the social environment was not conducive to recovery from these violence-induced conditions. (Hodgetts, 2003) In this context, there was much scepticism about the EFP Program and its ability to achieve its main objectives: to create, in and between the participating school communities, *a culture of peace*, a *culture of healing,* and a *culture of excellence*. Since its inception in 2000, the EFP program in Bosnia and Herzegovina has been introduced into the curricula of all 1000+ schools (K–12) with over 500,000 students and 70,000 BiH teachers and educators.

Outcome

The Education for Peace (EFP) pilot project was successful and we were invited to introduce the EFP program to another 106 schools with approximately 5,000 teachers and staff, 80,000 students, and tens of thousands of parents/guardians. This task was accomplished over a period of four years (2003–2007). The EFP Program is now (2014) being gradually introduced into all BiH schools. During this period, based on the lessons learned from this massive experience, the research that was conducted and after review of the current literature on peace education, a comprehensive and integrated EFP curriculum was developed. The curriculum comprises eleven volumes.

The criteria by which the EFP Program is evaluated are intended to determine to what extent it has accomplished its three main objectives—to create *a culture of peace,* a *culture of healing* (from the adverse effects of conflict, violence and war), *and a culture of excellence* (academic behavioral and relational)in the institutions and environments (family, school, community agencies, etc.) in which the program is introduced. The following excerpts are representative of the wide range of personal and institutional evaluation of the EFP Program. These statements reflect the appreciation of the participants not only about being educated for peace but also about being educated regarding self-knowledge and the ability to create unity in the context of extreme diversity.

> "The children all over the world are in need of peace and security. On the occasion of the Summit devoted to the children, we recommend this program [EFP] to all the nations for consideration, as a model of society oriented towards peace, cooperation and development."– From a letter addressed to the Special Session of the United Nations General Assembly on Children (8–10 May 2002) by the Government of Bosnia and Herzegovina,through its Mission to UN in New York

> "This invaluable project was conceived in such a way that the soul-searching process of reflection which the participants undergo as the project unfolds – be they pupils, teachers, parents, administrators, ordinary school workers – results, largely speaking, as we have ascertained ourselves, in a heightened holistic awareness of the war period and its tragic consequences and indeed triggers the desire amongst them to become authentic peace-makers and precisely provides them with the necessary tools to achieve this goal…."– Claude Kieffer Senior Education Advisor, Office of the High Representative, BiH (2002)

> "As a result of participating in the EFP project, my way of teaching has changed, my relationships with students have changed and my relationship with my family has changed… all for the better." – Teacher, Secondary School, BiH (2001)

> "In this project we learned many new things: new approaches to resolving conflicts, how to create our own lives and how to make our own decisions. But the most important thing that we learned is to be at peace with ourselves and teach other people to be peaceful. Our society doesn't have many projects like this."– Student, High School, BiH (2002)

> "This project has changed our vision and worldview. I feel that the vision of every teacher and student in this school has been in some way changed through this project." – Literature Teacher, High School, BiH (2002)

> "As an American peace worker, I often find myself internally torn asunder by my role in a country (and a world) that seems to thrive in a state of violent conflict. The question I constantly wrestle with is: How do I bridge the gap between living out Martin Luther King, Jr.'s call to righteous indignation and Gandhi's challenge to "be the change I wish to see in the world"? …For the past few months, I have been taught that conflict is unavoidable and is only destructive when one is unable to transform it in positive ways. Dr.Danesh's rejection of this model and his proposal of UNITY as an alternative were quite invigorating. Personally, I find that working toward unity is much more life-giving than is conflict transformation." – Robert Rivers, MA student, European University Centre for Peace and Conflict Studies (2005)

> "EFP provides a framework for achieving an advanced human society that is both practical and universal…I have always heard people say that 'education is the key' to creating a culture of peace. Before now though, no one seemed to have the right key that would actually open the lock. A 'Culture of Peace' is no longer an empty concept for me."– Yolanda Cowan, Rotary World Peace Scholar, Studying in Paris and an Intern with in EFP Balkans (2004–2005)

> "The EFP experience for the faculty of Boulder Prep was quite interesting. As the faculty began to see how students being taught from the perspective of peace in all subjects could cause dramatic changes in the outlook of our youth, the faculty themselves began to experience the beginnings of a paradigm shift. A paradigm shift, the whole world but especially our schools worldwide need to experience." – Andre Adeli, Co-Founder and Co-Director, Boulder Preparatory High School Boulder, Colorado, USA (2006)

> "I believe the uniqueness of the EFP Project, alongside its successful outcomes, can also inform educational policy and curriculum in many other communities in crisis; for example, Indigenous and minority communities." Sophia Close, researcher from Australia (2005–2006)

Finally, it is instructive to remember the wise counsel of Mahatma Gandhi: "If we are to teach real peace in this world and if we are to carry on a real war against war, we shall have to begin with the children." (Accessed, 2014)

Oportunidades

Toward Victory over Poverty

In 1994, President Ernesto Zedillo of Mexico asked Santiago Levy, a professor of economics at Boston University, to propose a program for the help of the poor, particularly in the hardest hit rural regions of the country. Professor Levy proposed a program based on *conditional cash transfers* to poor families—on condition that the family improves its nutritional and hygiene standards, particularly those of the children; that the children attend school regularly; and that the children are provided with such necessities as shoes, clothing, and a reasonable living environment through home improvement. Because of the prevalence of authoritarian worldview, machismo, and oppressive practices on the part of men, it was stipulated that the women in the family would receive the cash and spend it.

This simple and elegant program, initially called *Progresso* and later renamed *Oportunidades* by President Fox, started in 1997, after a successful pilot project. Because of its success on a very large scale and over a reasonably long time, Oportunidades has been studied by many researchers, governments, and international organizations such as the World Bank. This body of research and surveys indicates clearly that the program has had remarkable success. The number of poor families and the episodes of sickness and malnutrition have decreased, while the rates of school enrolment and vaccination have increased. These are excellent results and the Government of Mexico is satisfied enough with the program to spend approximately 3.8 billion dollars annually on it. Another unique aspect of Oportunidades is that, according to the director of the program, 97 percent of the budget is given to the beneficiaries. The principles of Oportunidades have been adopted in similar programs in more than 20 countries, including Bangladesh, Honduras, Jamaica, Argentina, Turkey, and the United States.

Several concerns have emerged, including the effectiveness of the program among the urban poor, the low standards of education that students receive, and the slow rate of change from machismo/authoritarian attitudes, beliefs and practices to more democratic and less conflicted relationships, particularly between men and women in the context of the family, school, and community. (Sedesol 2014, World Bank 2014, Oxford Journals 2014)

I feel that the effectiveness of this outstanding program will be greatly enhanced if it were coupled with a comprehensive education reform program based on the principles of peace, such as those offered by the EFP Curriculum.

These two programs together address the two interrelated issues of poverty and violence that have brought, and continue to bring, such havoc to the lives of the majority of humanity and particularly to the world's children and youth.

Fulfilling Our Responsibilities

Now, we have arrived at the most consequential of all issues regarding the welfare of the world's children—**action**. Who is going to assume responsibility and act? It is evident that we *all* have to be involved. Leaders in all segments of the world society—governments, religions, international institutions, financial institutions, academia, the media, all leaders at all levels—have sacred, urgent, and unique responsibilities with regard to the welfare of children. It is clear that we have to simultaneously focus on both short-term and long-term programs of action. Children in the midst of poverty, disease, and violence need immediate and effective attention and everyone has an opportunity and a duty to be involved in this task. At the same time, families and adults, and local and national institutions in every society have to bring themselves to account with regard to the treatment of children in their midst. However, the greatest responsibility belongs to the world's wealthy and powerful nations and their citizens. To a significant degree, these populations—themselves and/or their ancestors, directly or indirectly—are responsible for the poverty, disease, violence, and destruction prevalent in many parts of the world. Many of the wealthy and powerful nations have a history of colonialism and slavery. Many of them have benefited and continue to benefit from the natural resources of the poor countries of the world. A significant number of these countries manufacture and sell instruments of war and destruction to unscrupulous government leaders in many parts of the globe. We in the West and the North owe it to the children and parents of the East and the South to act. And we owe it to our own children to improve the lot of other children. This is so because we all belong to one human family and the misfortune of any member is the misfortune of all. The poor and impoverished countries of the world also have to assume their own responsibility and begin to heal their trampled souls with courageous deeds of care, compassion, and fairness toward each other and their children. The chart given here summarizes the main areas of responsibility for short- and long-term programs aimed at the betterment of the condition of the world's children.

To conclude, I wish to call to mind this statement by President Barak Obama, who in a speech on June 15, 2008, said:

> Life doesn't count for much unless you're willing to do your small part to leave our children—all of our children—a better world. Even if it's difficult.Even if the work seems great.Even if we don't get very far in our lifetime. (Obama, 2008)

THE CHALLENGE		ASSUMING RESPONSIBILITY	RESULTS
S H O R T T E R M	**VIOLENCE** End violence at:	**WHO IS REPONSIBLE?**	**Trans- formation** from a **C U L T U R E of C O N F L I C T**
	- Home	- Family (****) Government (***)	
	- School	- School(****) Government (****) Family (****)	
	- Community	- Civil Society (****) Religion (****) Business (***)	
	- Internet/Media	- Government (****) Producers (****) Parents (****)	
	POVERTY: END - Hunger	- Governments, International Community, Civil Society, Religion, Business, Individuals (all ****)	
	- Disease	- Governments, International Community, Civil Society, Religion, Business, Individuals (all ****)	
	- Illiteracy	- Governments, International Community, Civil Society, Religion, Business, Individuals (all ****)	
	- Homelessness	- Governments, International Community, Civil Society, Religion, Business, Individuals (all ****)	
	- Exploitation	- Governments, International Community, Civil Society, Religion, Business, Individuals (all ****)	
		- Governments, International Community, Civil Society, Religion, Business, Individuals (all ****)	

LONG TERM	**PEACE-BASED EDUCATION:** - Unity-Based Worldview - Unity in Diversity - Gender Equality - Peace-Based Governance **PROSPERITY:** - Peace-Based Economy - End of Poverty - Environmental Protection	**ALL ARE EQUALLY RESPONSIBLE** (****) School, Government, Family, Religion, Media, International Community, Academia, Civil Society, Individuals, etc. **ALL ARE RESPONSIBLE, SPECIALLY:** Government (****) Business (****) International Community (****) Media (***), Academia (***), Civil Society (***) Individuals (****)	to a **CIVILIZATION** of **PEACE**

Fig. 2.Proposed short-term and long-term plans for the betterment of the condition of the world's children. The asterisks (*) denote the levels of responsibility.

References

'Abdu'l-Bahá, *Some Answered Questions,* Wilmette, Illinois: Bahá'í Publishing Trust, 1987, 7.

—. quoted in J. E. Esslemont, (1987). *Bahá'u'lláh and the New Era.* 5th rev. ed. Wilmette, Illinois: Bahá'í Publishing Trust, 1987. 149.

Barker, Francis (1993), *The Culture of Violence: Tragedy and History,* Chicago: University of Chicago Press.

Danesh, H.B. (1995). *The Violence-Free Family: Building Block of a Peaceful Civilization*, Ottawa: Bahá'í Studies Publications.

—. (2006). "Towards an Integrative Theory of Peace Education," *Journal of Peace Education* 3.1: 55–78.

—. (2008a). "Unity-Based Peace Education," *Encyclopedia of Peace Education,* edited by Monisha Bajaj, Charlotte, North Carolina: Information Age Publishing, pp.147–56.

—. (2008b). "The Education for Peace Integrative Curriculum: Concepts, Contents, and Efficacy," *Journal of Peace Education* 5. 2 (September 2008): pp. 157–73.

—. (2008c). "Creating a Culture of Healing in Multiethnic Communities: An Integrative Approach to Prevention and Amelioration of Violence-Induced Conditions," *Journal of Community Psychology* 36. 6 (2008): 814–32.

—. (2011). Human Needs Theory, Conflict, and Peace: In Search of an Integrated Model. In D. J. Christie (Ed.), *Encyclopedia of Peace Psychology*. Hoboken, New Jersey: Wiley-Blackwell.

—. Editor (2011a), *Education for Peace Reader,* Vancouver, EFP Press.

Dawkins, Richard (2006). *The Selfish Gene (30th Anniversary edition).* New York City: Oxford University Press.

Dewey, John (1897) 'My pedagogic creed', *The School Journal*, Volume LIV, Number 3 (January 16, 1897), pages 77-80. [Also available in the *informal education archives*, http://infed.org/mobi/john-dewey-my-pedagogical-creed/. Retrieved:12 Nov. 2014].

Gandhi,Mahatma.http://www.light-a-fire.net/quotations/authors/mahatma-gandhi/. (Accessed 9 July 2013).

Gould, Stephen Jay (1990). "Caring Groups and Selfish Genes". *The Panda's Thumb: More Reflections in Natural History*. Harmondsworth: Penguin Books. pp. 72–78.

Harrington, Michael (1962) *The Other America,*Scribner, New York City (1997 Edition)

Hodgetts, Geoffrey et al. (2003). “Post-traumatic Stress Disorder among Family Physicians in Bosnia and Herzegovina,” *Family Practice* 20, 4 (2003): 489–491.

Lewis, Oscar (1975) *Five Families; Mexican Case Studies In The Culture Of Poverty*, Basic Books; New York, New Edition.

Lewis, Oscar (1979). *The Children Of Sánchez, Autobiography Of A Mexican Family* , 1961 Vintage, New York (1979 Edition)

Moynihan, Daniel Patrick (1965) *The Negro Family* (Moynihan Report), http://www.dol.gov/oasam/programs/history/webid-meynihan.htm (Accessed July 9, 2013)

Obama, Barak (2008), http://www.notable-quotes.com/c/children_quotes.html. (Accessed 9 July 2013).

Oxford Journal. http://wber.oxfordjournals.org/content/early/2013/01/04/wber.lhs032.abstract (Accessed 15 February 2014)

Pope John Paul II, http://www.brainyquote.com/quotes/quotes/p/popejohnpa138667.html (Accessed 9 July 2013).

Rosenberg, Tina (2008). *A Payoff Out of Poverty?* New York Times (December 21, 2008)

SEDESOL (Secretaria de Desarrollo Social). http://evaluacion.oportunidades.gob.mx:8010/index1.php (Accessed 9 July 2013

Sterelny, Kim (2007). *Dawkins vs. Gould: Survival of the Fittest.* Cambridge: Icon Books. p. 83.

UNICEF, http://www.unicef.org/protection/index_bigpicture.html, Accessed December 6, 2008

UNESCO (1996).*From a Culture of Violence to a Culture of Peace,* published by UNESCO Publishing, 1996. Original from the University of Michigan, digitized 22 October 2008

Wilson, David Sloan; Wilson, Edward O. (2007). "Rethinking the Theoretical Foundations of Sociobiology". *The Quarterly Review of Biology* 82 (4): 327–348.

World Bank. http://www.worldbank.org/projects/P115067/support-oportunidades-project?lang=en (Accessed 15 February 2014)

CHAPTER THREE

WHY CHILDREN'S RIGHTS MATTER

JOHN WALL

The Italian educator Maria Montessori once said, "I keep pointing at the child, they keep staring at my finger." I want to show that the same is often the case when we point to children's rights. Instead of applying adult rights to children, we should transform, in the light of childhood, the very idea of human rights.

That children's rights matter is obvious, hopefully. But *why*? What should rights do for children that can't be done in other ways? This is a pressing question for us for at least two reasons. First, the very notion of "rights" was never intended by its European Enlightenment framers to apply to children; indeed, children were explicitly excluded from them. And second, even as "rights" have become increasingly afforded to children over the past century, both in national laws and internationally, they have consistently fallen short in their aim of providing children full social citizenship. The danger of applying human rights talk to children lies in sounding good but not really making much difference, which is yet another way of marginalizing the third of humanity who happen to be children.

In order to suggest a more child-centered view of human rights here, I first indulge in some philosophical groundwork and examine why modernity's invention of rights excluded children on purpose. Then I chart how the path of international children's rights agreements in the twentieth century tried to struggle against this exclusion. Finally, I suggest a postmodern way to understand children's rights that actually responds to the experiences and voices of children, and I illustrate it in relation to the theme of giving children a voice through families. I call this new perspective "childism": a term which—in analogy, for example, to feminism, womanism, and environmentalism—is meant to call for a fundamental cultural, social, and political shift, this time in light of childhood (Wall 2010).

Why Human Rights Historically Excluded Children

We can understand, first, why children have been the major human group excluded from human rights in history if we look into the ideas of the three white European men who created our ideas of human rights in the first place.

First, the seventeenth century Englishman John Locke, who invented the modern rights theory itself, as well as the bases for new democracies in England and then my own country, the United States, grounds rights on the following: A right is the natural liberty of each individual in society to pursue their own "self-preservation," that is, their own "property" or life, liberty, and estate. It is society's guarantee that you will be free to pursue your own interests unmolested by others. But, according to Locke, the one group that must therefore be excluded is precisely children, because children, he thought, lack the rational capacities to be able to pursue their own self-interest for themselves. Children should not be their own "property" but rather what he calls the "temporary property" of their parents, who are solely responsible for furthering children's interests on children's behalf. This argument is still sometimes made today, and it reflects what I would call a longstanding "developmental" perspective on children, which dates back at least to Aristotle, in which children are viewed as "blank slates," "white pages," or mere "potentialities" and so only gradually join rational society as they mature into adulthood (Locke 1823: 107–108, 116–117, 126–133, 138, 146–147, 159–161, and 179–180; and Locke 1989: 83, 105, and 138–39).

Second, the early eighteenth century French social thinker Jean-Jacques Rousseau argues somewhat differently that human rights exist to include in social governance the active participation of all citizens. An inspiration behind the egalitarian ideals of the French Revolution, he envisions a just society as one based, not just on the pursuit of self-interest, but on everyone having the right to contribute toward what he calls "the general will." But this participatory ideal is thought, once again, necessarily to exclude children. For Rousseau views children (and societies) in what I would call a "bottom-up" way—found also, for example, in early Christianity and later Romanticism—in which life starts out not blank but in a state of positive natural purity, innocence, and giftedness, on which all goodness in society is built. But precisely for this reason, he claims, children should be kept apart from the corrupting influences of public life for as long as possible, so that they may be nurtured into the necessary moral strength in the private sanctity of the home. And so, as has also been the case for women and other groups, children are elevated to an ethereal pedestal that also sentimentalizes and sequesters them, including from the realm of civic participation (Rousseau 1979: 34 and 37; and Rousseau 1947: I.2, I.4, I.6, and II.1.).

Finally, the late eighteenth century German philosopher Immanuel Kant claimed, somewhat differently again, that rights are based on humanity's capacity for what he calls "autonomy" or rational self-legislation. Human beings are on one level desiring, wanting, instinctual animals; but on another level they are capable of regulating their animal natures according to the guiding stars of universal moral laws. Rights function, as per this view, to protect our dignity as autonomous ends in ourselves against being used as mere means to our own or others' wants. Children, however, are once again the sole major exception. For in Kant's view, children have not yet learned to discipline their baser impulses through higher civilized principles. They may be owed a certain dignity in not being used by others as mere means, but they cannot yet be considered rational rights-bearing subjects in themselves, capable of directing their own actions rationally. Kant takes what I would call a "top-down" approach to children—also found, for example, in Plato, Augustine, John Calvin, and still today—in which children's unruly and even sinful natures are considered to make them unsuitable for involvement in civilized social order (Kant 1960: 6 and 11; Kant 1974: paras. 28-29; and Kant 1990: 47).

As we can see, then, the very architectural foundations of human rights are thoroughly adult-centered. Women, minorities, and other historically marginalized groups have at least gradually been able to fight for inclusion in these kinds of rights frameworks by proving their own independent rational capacities. But children have continued to be denied what Hannah Arendt has called the very "right to have rights" almost by philosophical necessity.

Twentieth century children's rights agreements

Nevertheless, as I would now like to show, the past century has seen a countervailing struggle to extend human rights to children in practice. This movement effectively constitutes an implicit critique of the traditional moral groundings rights. Nowhere is it more visible and powerful than in the three major international children's rights agreements produced by the League of Nations and its successor the United Nations. In fact, the first of these, the 1924 Geneva Declaration of the Rights of the Child, was the first ever global human rights document. And the last of them, the 1989 Convention on the Rights of the Child, is humanity's most widely ratified legal agreement of all time. How does this mounting children's rights struggle challenge its own Enlightenment bases?

The 1924 Declaration is in fact a very simple document that contains only five rights, which are almost exclusively what have been called "provision" rights, or rights for children to receive national and international aid. Included here are such rights as to the means for normal development, adequate nutrition and healthcare, priority in disaster relief, and a basic education. Provision rights are more or less based on Locke's idea that individuals are owed the basic means for their own self-preservation, what is now called children's "best interests." Such rights appear to have been extended to children in recognition of the fact that children cannot have their interests supported by their families alone, but, as had also been recognized at the time for women and laborers, are in part dependent also, especially in today's complex societies, on the active support of larger social systems.

The second major international children's rights agreement is the 1959 Declaration of the Rights of the Child. This Declaration expands children's rights to ten, roughly half of which are similar kinds of provision rights as in 1924, the other half consisting of a new kind of what can be called "protection" rights, or rights *against* being done violence and harm by others. These include children's rights against racial, sexual, and other kinds of discrimination; neglect, cruelty, and exploitation; separation from parents; trafficking; and labor. This new dimension reflects the spirit of the United Nations' founding 1948 Universal Declaration of Human Rights, which is a chiefly protection rights document intended to respond to the great horrors of World War II, where humanity, and especially children, had been so clearly exposed as vulnerable to social disorder and exploitation. But in a deeper, philosophical sense, its added protection rights express Kant's notion that rights exist to guard against violence to human dignity. They are now extended to children as evidently unable to be protected by their parents alone and as open as anyone else to public harm, if not more so. And this right to protection also gets extended in many societies, starting in the 1970s, against abuse from members of a child's own family.

But by far the most extensive international children's rights agreement is of course the United Nation's 1989 Convention on the Rights of the Child, which contains 40 distinct children's rights that are spelled out in much greater detail. What is interesting for our purposes about this Convention, which has helped prompt a sea change in global attitudes toward children, is that it adds yet a third layer of ethical complexity. It contains approximately 18 provision rights (including all those previously mentioned as well as such rights as to an official identity and an adequate standard of living), plus approximately 16 protection rights (adding also protections such as against torture, degrading punishment and drafting into armed conflict). But it also contains an entirely new category of so-called "participation" rights which had been entirely absent from previous agreements, that is, rights to act and have a voice in society on one's own behalf. These six participation rights, briefly stated, are to be heard; freedom of expression; freedom of thought, conscience, and religion; freedom of association and assembly; privacy; and access to the use of mass media. According to our historical analysis, these chiefly reflect Rousseau's notion of human rights as bottom-up inclusions in the shaping of societies. They are extended now to children on the view, chiefly promoted by the childhood studies movement, that children should be allowed not just to receive society's aid and protection but also to act for themselves as social citizens (James and Prout 1990; Jenks 1996; Mouritsen and Qvortrup 2002; Pufall and Unsworth 2004).

What this twentieth century development of children's rights shows overall is not just that rights language *can* be extended to children but that the more this is done, the more it requires combining *all three kinds* of traditional human rights bases. None of the well-worn ideas of rights alone can capture what children truly call for. Rather, extending rights to children involves thinking of rights themselves in increasingly complex ways.

Rights as responsibilities

However, as I would like now to suggest, fitting these diverse kinds of rights together requires us to make a fundamental transition from modernistic *individual autonomy* to a post-modernistic ethic of what I will call *interdependent responsibility*. From an Enlightenment point of view, rights and responsibilities are simply opposed: the one gives freedoms while the other binds us together. Or, put differently, the one is public and legal while the other is private and familial. But children teach us more than any other group that these are false dichotomies. What truly makes us human is not independence (or its opposite, dependence) but rather the basic intersubjective experience of interdependence. Rights in the light of childhood are both public and private expressions of responsibility toward each other. Their purpose is to expand humanity's responsiveness to its own constituting differences (Levinas 1969; Ricoeur 1992; Derrida 1995; Kearney 2003; Wall 2005). From birth onward, each human being is at once constructed by larger social worlds and uniquely constructive of them, so that every one of us fully belongs to a dynamic circle of social creativity. Children may not be as autonomous as adults, but they are every bit as socially other. The question for rights is how to expand the interdependent human circle ever more other-responsively.

The 1989 Convention, while far from perfect, helps us to imagine human rights as responsibilities in practice. By integrating a complex diversity of kinds of rights into a single cohesive document, it recognizes that children—and by extension all of us—are simultaneously dependent and independent, passive and active, receiving and contributing members of social worlds. Each of us belongs to interdependent networks of received developmental supports, imposed top-down protections, and active bottom-up opportunities for agency. Together, but not separately, these interlocking trajectories create dynamic societies capable of expanding human mutual responsibilities rather than contracting into exclusions and hegemonies.

Thus, for example, for children and adults both, provision rights such as to healthcare and education are best understood, not merely as handouts of aid, but as social responses to different kinds of social interdependency. Protection rights such as against violence and exploitation are not simply guards against individual harm, but mutual supports against social exclusion. And participation rights such as to freedom of speech and assembly are not just expressions of personal will but means for expanding the construction of societies by different others. Children may have less experience traversing such social circles, and adults therefore have comparatively wider social responsibilities. But all human beings, child and adult both, are owed the right to distinct and diverse responsiveness from their societies and have the obligation to respond to others in society themselves. Our responsibility as interdependent beings is to increase responsiveness to one another over time.

Rights in families

Let me end with an illustration from the realm of children's rights in families. For while the majority of the rights contained in the Convention on the Rights of the Child are *not* related to families, it is not often noted that many of them—and I count seven—centrally are. These seven deal with children's relations to family life on all three sides of the rights circle. There are four provision rights: to parental direction (Article 14.2), involvement from *both* parents (18.1), social aid being directed through parents (27.2), and parental teaching about rights themselves (5). There are two protection rights: against children's separation from their own family (except in cases of abuse) (9.1), and against abuse or neglect *within* families (19.1). And there is one family participation right: to take part in the privacy of a family home (16.1) Other Convention rights of course also impact family life indirectly: rights such as to education and healthcare, against discrimination and labour, and to freedom of expression.

This complex interdependency of family-related child rights simply cannot be explained on the Enlightenment model of rights-holders as autonomous individuals. Rather, children have rights in families as both passive and active members of an interdependent family circle. Receiving parental provision and support is inextricably bound up with rights not to be abused and to participate in family functioning. In turn, protections against neglect and violence are necessary for living in a developmentally supportive family environment and one in which a child's active voice is encouraged. And being free to participate in a home environment also requires being able to receive parental support and to be guarded against parental and societal exploitation. The fundamental reason why children *and* adults have rights within families is that families are one of the most important ways in which human beings take responsibility for each other as different others. Families are sites of expanding responsibility which are also training grounds for children's and adults' capabilities for even more expanded responsibility in society.

Conclusion

The language of "human rights" does not say everything that needs to be said about children, children's voices, or children's roles in families. But what it does say—or *can* say—is that children are absolutely full human beings whose diversity and differences deserve society's and families' dynamic responses. We will not get to this ideal of treating children with true humanity through traditional ways of understanding rights. Rather, the very grounds of human rights will have to be reimagined through a new childism that can help reconstruct societies around not just modernistic freedoms or pre-modernistic dependencies, but rather post-modernistic interdependent responsibilities. It is this kind of cultural and moral transformation that children's rights are in a position to effect.

References

Derrida, Jacques (1995), *The Gift of Death*, trans. David Wills. Chicago: The University of Chicago Press.

James, Alison and Alan Prout, eds. (1990), *Constructing and Reconstructing Childhood: New Directions in the Sociology of Childhood.* New York: Falmer Press.

Jenks, Chris, *Childhood.* New York: Routledge, 1996.

Kant, Immanuel (1960), *Education*, trans. Annette Churton. Ann Arbor, MI: The University of Michigan Press.

—. (1974), *The Science of Right*, trans. W. Hastie. Clifton, N.J.: A. M. Kelley.

—. (1990), *Foundations of the Metaphysics of Morals*, trans. Lewis White Beck, Second Edition. Englewood Cliffs, NJ: Prentice-Hall.

Kearney, Richard (2003), *Strangers, Gods, and Monsters: Interpreting Otherness*. New York: Routledge.

Levinas, Emmanuel (1969), *Totality and Infinity: An Essay on Exteriority*, trans. Alphonso Lingis. Pittsburgh, PA: Duquesne University Press.

Locke, John (1823), *Two Treatises of Government*, from *The Works of John Locke*, New Edition, Vol. V. London: W. Sharpe and Son.

—. (1989), *Some Thoughts Concerning Education*, in J. W. and J. S. Yolton (eds.), *The Clarendon Edition of the Works of John Locke*. New York: Oxford University Press.

Mouritsen, Flemming and Jens Qvortrup, eds. (2002), *Childhood and Children's Culture*. Odense, Denmark: University Press of Southern Denmark.

Pufall, Peter B. and Richard P. Unsworth, eds. (2004), *Rethinking Childhood.* New Brunswick, NJ: Rutgers University Press.

Ricoeur, Paul (1992), *Oneself as Another*, trans. Kathleen Blamey. Chicago: University of Chicago Press.

Rousseau, Jean-Jacques (1979), *Emile, or On Education*, trans. Allan Bloom. New York: Basic Books.

—. (1947), *The Social Contract*, trans. Charles Frankel. New York: Hafner.

Wall, John (2005), *Moral Creativity: Paul Ricoeur and the Poetics of Possibility*. New York: Oxford University Press.

—. (2010), *Ethics in Light of Childhood*.Washington, DC: Georgetown University Press.

CHAPTER FOUR

LOOKING AT THE SEXUAL VICTIMIZATION OF CHILDREN FROM A DEVELOPMENTAL PERSPECTIVE

JANIS WOLAK

This chapter is adapted from the work on developmental victimology by David Finkelhor, Director, Crimes against Children Research Center (CCRC), University of New Hampshire (Finkelhor, 2007).

Child sexual victimization has become increasingly recognized as a source of harm to children, and as a global phenomenon. Sexual victimization can take many forms, including sexual abuse or exploitation in the children's own homes. This may be in the form of incest, sexual touching, exposure to pornography, or child pornography production. When such victimization occurs in homes, family members are often perpetrators. Sexual victimizations can also occur in schools, residential care settings, workplaces, neighborhoods, and communities. In such settings, abuse may be committed by adults who teach, work with, employ, or have other positions of trust or authority with children. Sexual victimization can also happen at the hands of peers, particularly among adolescents. In addition, children may be the target of commercial sexual exploitation in enterprises such as prostitution, child pornography production, and child trafficking for sexual purposes.

Further, some forms of sexual victimization involve nonviolent acts that would ordinarily be acceptable between adults, but are deemed victimization in the case of children because of their immaturity and dependency (e.g., an adult who seduces a young adolescent into sexual activity). Other forms of sexual abuse, however, involve violence and coercion that would be victimizing even with a nondependent adult. Examples are rape and abuse of authority.

The importance of a developmental perspective on child sexual victimization

Childhood is a period of enormous changes in size, strength, cognitive capacities, gender differentiation, relationships, and social environments—all of which affect the potential for sexual victimization. Moreover, these developmental changes interact with one another, so their impact is not simple or straightforward. For example, children do not necessarily become safer from sexual abuse or exploitation as they become older and stronger. Rather, the places in which sexual victimizations occur, the identities of perpetrators, the nature of victim/abuser relationships, and the responses of victims change as children mature. A developmental perspective is helpful in understanding both the nature of sexual victimization and its impact on children.

Two separate domains of developmental impact

Child development impacts two separate domains of child sexual victimization. The first concerns developmental aspects of the *risk* of being victimized. The types of victimization that children suffer depend on their age and level of development in very basic ways. Children become progressively less dependent as they get older. Consequently, younger children suffer a greater proportion of victimization at the hands of caretakers and other intimates than at the hands of strangers. This is because dependency-related victimization involving younger children also usually involves perpetrators who are caregivers and family members, the people on whom the responsibilities created by children's dependency status fall.

The second domain concerns the developmental aspects of the *impact* of sexual victimization. How children respond to victimization depends on capacities and vulnerabilities that are related to their developmental stage. General principles can be drawn about the nature of their reactions to abuse and the ways in which such reactions develop and change based on age and stage of development.

Developmental aspects of the *risk* of sexual victimization

Risk of sexual victimization varies by age, and certain domains affecting such risk also vary over the course of development. These domains can be divided into two subcategories: the characteristics of children themselves and the characteristics of the environments they inhabit. Characteristics of children, in turn, can be broken down into those affecting their likelihood of being targeted for victimization and those relating to their ability to protect themselves.

Characteristics of children

Over the course of development, children both acquire and lose characteristics that make them more or less likely to be targeted for sexual victimization. An obvious example is sexual maturation, which tends to make children, especially girls, more vulnerable to sexually motivated crimes. This statement about sexual maturation must be qualified, however, because pedophilic sex offenders target prepubescent victims, so the risk of victimization by these abusers is higher among younger children and decreases as they mature.

Children also change with age in their ability to protect themselves from sexual victimization. However, in terms of risk of sexual abuse, the changes in capacities for self-protection that occur as children get older are not uniform. For example, some of the urges and pressures to take risks (e.g., to drink, take drugs, or go to unsupervised parties) that characterize adolescence represent a decline in the capacity for self-protection. The risk of sexual victimization among teenage girls, in particular, may be affected by such relatively common, risky adolescent behaviors. Other factors also may interfere with children's abilities to protect themselves. For example, the types of intellectual or physical limitations that constitute developmental disabilities may compromise children's abilities to protect themselves. These also appear to be associated with increased risk of sexual abuse and may be a vulnerability that does not decrease with age for some potential victims. In addition, victimization itself seems to compromise children's capacities to resist subsequent victimization, perhaps by undermining their confidence, assertiveness, or ability to assess the trustworthiness of possible abusers.

A further consideration is that a child's age often affects not only the risk of sexual victimization but also the likelihood that the child will report the abuse. For example, it appears to be much more difficult for children younger than six to disclose sexual abuse than for those over age twelve. There may be several reasons for this. Younger children may be less able to articulate what has happened to them, have less understanding about what sexually abusive behaviors are, be more easily frightened or intimidated by abusers, and less able to remember incidents as they get older.

The role of gender in risk for victimization is another important factor. Developmental factors affect boys' and girls' risk for sexual victimization in different ways. An obvious example is rape, since sexual maturation results in a dramatic increase in the risk of this crime for girls and makes little difference in incidences involving boys. While girls are generally at a greater risk of sexual victimization, fewer boys may disclose abuse when it occurs. This may be because boys victimized by adult males become aware of the harsh discrimination against homosexual relationships and fear hurting their own reputations among peers.

Characteristics of environments

The environments in which children live, travel, and work change over the course of their development, dramatically affecting their risk for sexual victimization. However, the picture is not a simple one of children becoming more vulnerable as they move into less supervised environments. Rather, there is a complex pattern of change as children move into different environments. Cultural and socioeconomic considerations also play a role in this pattern. For example, when children are allowed to stay out at night, they may enter into higher risk environments. The age at which this happens varies widely, depending on cultural and other factors. In cultures where dating is allowed for young adolescent girls, they may be more vulnerable to rape because of the amount of time spent alone and unsupervised with adolescent boys. However, much sexual victimization of children and adolescents occurs within their own homes. For this reason, some children may be safer outside of their home environments.

That children have limited autonomy over their own environments is a key aspect in understanding children's sexual victimization. They are unable to choose their associates and often cannot regulate their contact with abusive contacts or find safety with capable guardians. Children cannot generally choose their family, neighborhood, or school. They cannot easily opt to leave settings that become threatening or dangerous. Their daily routine confines them to large, heterogeneous environments, including schools, where they may have direct and involuntary exposure to potential abusers. When children are employed, their jobs tend to involve undesirable hours and involuntary contact with the public in large, diverse places such as restaurants, shops, or delivery services.

As children acquire relatively greater control over their environments, their risk of sexual victimization seems to be less a matter of compulsory circumstances than of personal choices. Many different developmental processes seem to affect adolescent choices, including the formation of personal identities, acquisition of self-esteem, evolution of an individual style in interpersonal relationships, history of academic performance, prior experience of violence and abuse, and cultural and economic factors. Unfortunately, there has been a tendency in both professional and general thinking to overemphasize this single developmental pattern, which tends to result in the view that adolescents are largely responsible for their own victimization, while younger children are not.

However, there are many forms of sexual victimization, such as incest and other intrafamilial sexual assaults, which cannot be blamed on delinquent affiliations. Most importantly, the proposition that sexual victimization among teenagers stems primarily from adolescent tendencies to engage in risky behavior such as drinking and sexual experimentation fails to recognize much of the generally involuntary and high-risk nature of adolescent work, school and community environments.

Developmental aspects of the *impacts* of sexual victimization

There are many burgeoning developmental processes in childhood which are sensitive to disturbance, and the impact of sexual victimization on these processes needs to be systematically taken into account. To bring together the insights from what is known about the impacts of crime victimization and of child sexual abuse, two types of effects should be distinguished. The first is those specific to the trauma experience but without major developmental ramifications, which could be called localized effects. The second is impacts that could be called developmental, which reflect a disturbance in developmental processes.

Localized effects

Localized effects refer to such common symptoms after traumatic events as fearfulness, which is relatively frequent in sexually victimized children. Among children, localized effects may include the fear of returning to a place where victimization occurred, anxiety and wariness around adults who resemble the offender, nightmares, being upset by television depictions of sexual violence, and so forth. These symptoms can be called localized not only in the sense that they are short-term, which they often are, but also in the sense that they primarily affect behavior associated with the victimization experience and similar classes of experience.

Developmental impacts

In contrast, developmental impacts refer to deeper and more generalized types of effects, more specific to children, which result when the sexual victimization experience and its related trauma interfere with developmental tasks or distort their course. Developmental effects include the impairment of attachment among very young victims. Young children may also be more likely to experience dissociation, which is characterized by large memory losses and trance-like behavior. Other developmental impacts include lowered self-esteem, the adoption of highly sexualized modes of interpersonal relating, failure to acquire competence in peer relations, and, dissociation, self-injury, the use of drugs, or other dysfunctional methods to deal with anxiety.

Developmental effects are more likely to occur under a number of conditions. First, they are more likely to occur if the sexual victimization is repetitive and ongoing. Second, they are more likely to arise if the victimization dramatically changes the nature of the child's relationship with his or her primary support system. Sexual victimization by a parent obviously creates such interference, but similar effects may result when parents reject a child or become overprotective as a result of a sexual victimization. A third circumstance is when the victimization adds to other serious stressors, for instance, sexual abuse of a child who is simultaneously suffering from bereavement, parental divorce, poverty, or homelessness or has previously suffered from these. Finally, developmental effects may occur if, because of its timing or source, the victimization interrupts a crucial developmental transition. For example, if a girl who is just entering adolescence and beginning to date suffers a violent sexual assault, this may result in long-term issues.

A further related developmental factor is how a victim of sexual abuse or exploitation understands the events they suffered. For example, victims seem to be affected more by victimizations during which they believed they were going to be seriously injured or felt helpless and out of control. However, this process of understanding, sometimes called "cognitive appraisal," goes through stages of development in childhood, during which it works very differently from the cognitive appraisal of adults. Younger children's appraisals of a sexual victimization may be largely taken from how their parents or other authoritative adults in their lives viewed the incident rather than from the objective nature of the event. This means that the developmental immaturity of young children does not necessarily increase the trauma of sexual victimization; it can buffer the impact as well. Buffering can also occur when a child does not fully understand the nature of a sexual victimization. This can happen because recognition of sexual abuse may require a variety of concepts that are not acquired until later in development. However, it is clear that even if a child does not recognize victimization when it occurs, recognition can occur when a child gets older and views the event in retrospect with negative consequences. Clinicians report that it can sometimes be extremely traumatizing for a child to recall or otherwise learn of an earlier, previously unremembered sexual victimization.

One important element of understanding, thought to be relevant to the impact of sexual victimization, is how the child attributes blame for the event. Victims of crimes and other misfortunes are believed to cope better if they do not blame themselves for what happened, which might otherwise cause them to see uncontrollable traits ("I'm too trusting") as the cause of the victimization. For young children, the most important issue may not be whether they think they have the power to prevent future victimization, but whether they think their parents or other caretakers do. In addition, more crucial than whether they blame themselves or others for the victimization (internal or external attribution), may be whether they think the cause of the victimization is constantly present across time and across situations (termed "stable" and "global" attributions).

References

Finkelhor, D. (2007) "Developmental Victimology," In Davis, R.C. et al. (Eds.) *Victims of Crime*, 3rd Edition, (Thousand Oaks, CA: Sage Publications, 2007).

CHAPTER FIVE

SOCIAL NETWORKING AS A NEXUS FOR ENGAGEMENT AND EXPLOITATION OF YOUNG PEOPLE

ETHEL QUAYLE AND MAX TAYLOR

Introduction

Social networking and social networking sites are extremely popular with youth and even children. Access to these sites are too often not supervised or monitored. As a result, these sites play a role in the engagement and exploitation of young people. This engagement is not limited to the realms of sexual deviance, but includes attempts to radicalize young people.

In the following pages, we focus on cybercrimes that relate to child pornography and online solicitation as well as radicalization efforts.

The relationship between sexual crimes against children and radicalization may seem obscure, although Weimann (2010) cites a news article by an unnamed "counter terrorism expert" which argues that terrorists use social networking sites such as Facebook, MySpace, and Second Life to target youth "in the same way a paedophile might look at those sites to potentially groom would-be victims." Others have sought to establish a relationship between terrorist activity and online sexual offences. For example, in 2008, The Times in the United Kingdom reported that "Secret coded messages are being embedded into child pornographic images, and paedophile [sic] websites are being exploited as a secure way of passing information between terrorists" (The Times, October 17, 2008). From a completely different perspective, in 2011, The Telegraph, another reputed UK newspaper, argued that Internet users were being spied upon in their own homes as the British Government used the threat of terrorism and the spread of child pornography to justify launching a dramatic expansion of surveillance society (The Telegraph, 30 May 2011). Is there anything beyond this rhetoric to link the two?

Young people as targets

An initial problem in exploring this is to define what "radicalized content" on the Internet might be, a problem that is not so apparent with child abuse images, for example. Taylor and Ramsey (2010) explore what might constitute such content, and note that themes such as "glorification of violence" and exploration of martyrdom are frequent qualities that seem to be used by Islamic extremist websites, for example; likewise, Nalton et al. (2011) have explored in some detail the role of the Internet in the propagation of Dissident Irish Republican material. While exact parallels between sexualized and sexual images and visual political material may be difficult to draw, effective commonalities might be established between the emotional valence of material such as beheading videos and child abuse images. At this level, as well as having a role in behavior change, commonalties may be apparent.

However, probably the most obvious link relates to the age of those targeted and their preferred online activities, reflecting not simply the significance of content, but also that of Internet process (Taylor and Quayle, 2006). Internet use by adolescents is increasing faster than that by any other age group (Jones & Fox, 2009) and this is the case not just for Western countries but those in the Middle East and Asia (e.g. Hui, 2010). Regan and Steeves (2010) have argued that there is a dynamic of surveillance and empowerment in the ways that young people have adopted or adapted online media in order to deepen social experiences, build community, and resist measures that seek to limit online speech and access to information. Social networking sites have been described by Marsico (2010) as the "fingerprints" of the twenty-first century, with Facebook, Twitter, and other sites becoming the "new commons: the place where you hang out, commiserate and gossip with your friends" (van Manen, 2010, p 1025).

The attraction of social networking sites for young people might, paradoxically, relate to the absence of freedom they enjoy compared to their parents and grandparents when they were young. Jewkes (2010) has suggested that the Internet can be thought of as a form of social retreat, providing "freedom of thought, freedom of expression, freedom to present an identity or indeed a multitude of identities, a *freedom of being*—quite unlike anything they have at their disposal in the physical world" (p 10). Gill (2008) has also argued that the enthusiastic adoption of social networking sites is in part driven by the erosion of children's freedoms in the physical world.

Social networks offer the opportunity to sustain local friendships that have already been established (Valkenburg & Peter, 2007), although there is some evidence in the United Kingdom that a substantial minority of young people (42% of a survey involving 2611 children aged 11–16) regularly interact socially online with people they have not met face to face (Sharples, Graber, Harrison & Logan, 2010), allowing for the creation and maintenance of extensive social networks of weak ties (Ellison, Steinfield & Lampe, 2007). Livingstone and Brake (2010) suggest that the limited research available links social networking with a range of content, contact, and conduct risks to children and young people, including some perpetrated by young people themselves.

In the context of online sexual crimes Mitchell, Finkelhor, Jones and Wolak (2010) from a mail survey of a nationally representative sample of over 2,500 local, state, and federal law enforcement agencies in the United States, found that social networking sites were used to initiate sexual relationships, to provide a means of communication between victim and offender, to access information about the victim, to disseminate information or pictures about the victim, and to get in touch with the victim's friends. A small number of these cases involved offenders who used social networking sites to distribute child pornography. This study suggested that the young people targeted were more likely to be older, and live in urban rather than rural communities. These authors concluded, however, that, "By teaching youth certain behaviors, such as not talking about sex with people they meet online and not posting sexual images of themselves, they can take this knowledge with them online, regardless of whether they are using an SNS, chat rooms, instant messaging, or whatever new technology is next on the horizon" (p. 190). However, not all children appear to be at risk and there is evidence that personal disclosure may heighten risk (Wolak, Finkelhor, Mitchell & Ybarra, 2008). Datan and Mislan (2010) in their analysis of three popular social networking sites (Facebook, MySpace, and Twitter) found that common user information on all three sites were name, age, gender, address, city, birthdate, photograph, sexual orientation, and relationship status.

Mitchell, Finkelhor & Wolak (2007) found that young people who send personal information, such as their name, telephone number, or pictures to unknown people or engage in online chat with people about sex are more likely to receive aggressive sexual solicitations (involving offline contact or attempts to meet). However Ybarra, Mitchell, Finkelhor and Wolak (2007) found in their survey that three-quarters of their sample of young people had not sent personal information to people they did not know offline, and only a small percentage (5%) talked online to unknown people about sex. Data from the EU Kids Online project would suggest that opportunities and risks are linked (Livingstone & Helsper, 2010) and the more skilled a young person is in the use of the Internet, the more he or she experiences both opportunities and risks.

Connectivity on social networking sites is expressed by creating a profile comparable to a personal home page (Boyd, 2007) that usually contains personally identifiable information, including one's name, contact information, and demographic data. To create connectedness, participants invite others to become their "friends" and respond to other's requests to be a "friend" to them. Users can post pictures and videos of themselves and their friends and "tag" or identify by name each person; and additional activity can be communicated to friends using a "news feed." While many studies have suggested a gender difference in information disclosure (e.g. Tufekci, 2008), research by Hoy and Milne (2010) of young adults (18–24 years) recruited through Facebook suggested that females were ambivalent about privacy and males unconcerned.

A study by Dowell, Burgess, and Cavaunaugh (2009) of a much younger age group (9–15 for boys and 11–15 for girls) using the Youth Internet Safety Survey, identified a cluster of risky Internet behaviors reported by the 20% of students who posted their pictures on the Internet. "These risky behaviors included *posting of personal information* (name of school, e-mail address, sending a picture of self), *corresponding online with an unknown person* (met person offline, developed relationship), *online initiated harassment* (playing jokes), *online-initiated sex sites,* and *overriding Internet filters or blocks"* (p 551). Data from an analysis of 131 Facebook profiles of young people aged 13–30 years suggested that most people, regardless of gender, give their full name, facial pictures, hometown, and e-mail addresses in their profiles (Taraszow, Aristodemou, Shitta, Laouris & Arsoy, 2010). However, males were more likely to disclose mobile phone numbers, home address, and Instant Messaging (IM) screen names.

It may seem obvious that disclosure of such information increases vulnerability. The US research from the University of New Hampshire research would suggest that most Internet-initiated sex crimes involve adult men who use the Internet to meet and seduce underage adolescents into sexual encounters and that in the majority of cases, victims are aware that they are conversing online with adults (Wolak et al., 2008). A comparison of survey data obtained from law enforcement agencies in 2000 and 2006 showed an increase in online predators, but an examination of the data indicated that this was largely accounted for by an increase in the number of young adults arrested (from 23% to 40%) (Wolak, Finkelhor & Mitchell, 2009).

Davidson et al. (2011) have proposed a definition of an online groomer as someone who has initiated online contact with a child with the intention of establishing a sexual relationship involving cybersex or sex with physical contact. Davidson et al. (2011) have also suggested that child grooming is a process that commences with sex offenders choosing a target area that is likely to attract children, and developing a bond as a precursor to abuse. The Internet offers speed and increases the range of contacts. A recent exploratory study was conducted by Briggs, Simon, and Simonsen (2010) of 51 people convicted of an Internet sex offence in which they attempted to entice an adolescent into a sexual relationship using an Internet chat room. The authors conclude that Internet chat room offenders constitute a separate group from other sex offenders and were characterized by less severe criminogenic factors. They hypothesized that chat room sex offenders typically avoided relationships and spent a significant amount of time in chat rooms as a primary social and sexual outlet. They also appeared to engage in other sexually compulsive behaviors. Briggs et al.'s data suggested two subgroups: a contact-driven group motivated to engage in offline sexual behavior, and a fantasy-driven group motivated to engage in cybersex, but without an express wish to meet young people offline.

However, the empirical research in relation to grooming or online solicitation is still sparse, and has largely focused on the behavior of the young person as opposed to the offending adult. It is also worth noting that in the University of New Hampshire research, both the 2000 and 2005 surveys indicated that nearly half of the sexual solicitations were initiated by other young people, somewhat challenging some of our assumptions about the nature of online grooming (Wolak et al. 2008).

This is in contrast to allegations such as those by Kim, Jeong, Kim, and So (2011) that many people join social networking sites to hunt for "sex victims" and that the number of such people is incredibly high. In part, this has been fueled by disclosures from social networking sites such as MySpace following a subpoena from the government of the United States, that their list of members contained the names of 90,000 convicted sex offenders who had used their real names. It is also the case that arrests of offenders in the United States who solicited undercover investigators saw the largest increase and constituted the largest proportion of arrests of online predators, with an estimated 3,100 arrests in 2006 (Wolak, Finkelhor & Mitchell, 2009).

Social networking and radicalization

Anxieties about young people and privacy have been termed a "technopanic response" by Harris (2010), who argues that one truth about young people's use of the Internet is that they are active participants in shaping their online experience. However, Livingstone and Brake (2010) caution that young people's agency should not be overstated as their practices are constrained by their degree of digital literacy and by the technical designs of social networking sites.

However, the use of such sites in the radicalization of youth has provoked considerable interest. Weimann (2010) has asserted that post-modern terrorists are taking advantage of the fruits of globalization and modern technology, with 90 percent of terrorist activity on the Internet taking place using social networking tools which act as a virtual firewall to help safeguard the identities of those who participate. "Popular social networking websites are another means of attracting potential members and followers. These types of communities are growing increasingly popular all over the world, especially among younger demographics. Jihadist terrorist groups especially target youth for propaganda, incitement and recruitment purposes… There are numerous Facebook groups declaring support for paramilitary and nationalist groups that the US government has designated as terrorist organizations, such as Hezbollah, Hamas, the Turkish Revolutionary People's Army, and the Liberation Tigers of Tamil Eelam (LTTE). The majority of these groups have open pages and anyone interested can read the information, look at discussion boards, click on links to propaganda videos, and join the group" (Weimann, 2010, p 49).

In 2009, the Homeland Security Institute prepared a report for the US Department of Homeland Security, Science and Technology Directorate. The report acknowledged the Internet as an important resource for disseminating terrorist propaganda and instructions to young persons who might not otherwise have direct contact with group recruiters or supporters. The accessibility and perceived anonymity of the Internet has offered terrorists (as with those with a sexual interest in children, Taylor & Quayle, 2003) a variety of media for disseminating propaganda along with dedicated websites targeting young people. This has led to notions of "self-radicalization" through the use of the Internet. An example of this is Roshonara Choudhary, who attacked the UK Member of Parliament Stephen Timms on 14 May, 2010. She had no known contact with any radical Islamic organizations, and appeared to have been motivated to carry out this attack wholly as a result of her accessing Internet material. She reportedly told police that "…she had wanted to die as a martyr after watching more than 100 hours of video sermons from the extremist cleric Anwar al-Awlaki which she had come upon on the Internet." (Guardian, http://www.guardian.co.uk/uk/2010/nov/04/stephen-timms-attack-roshonara-choudhry). She found all these videos on YouTube.

Another example of such radicalization can be seen in the case of Hammaad Munshi. Munshi was reported to have become obsessed by terrorism at the age of 15 when, instead of revising for his exams, he became preoccupied with surfing jihadist websites and distributing material related to wiping out non-Muslims. He was arrested at the age of 16 when walking home from his school in West Yorkshire in the United Kingdom and was subsequently found guilty at London's Blackfriars Crown Court of making a record of information likely to be useful in terrorism. It was suggested that his mentor was "Aabid Hussain Khan, 23, a leading 'cyber terrorist' who radicalized impressionable Muslims and encouraged them to attend military terror camps in Pakistan" (The Mail Online, 19 August, 2008).

An example of the kind of media involved is a website created by the Palestinian group Hamas, which targets young children through the use of cartoon characters (http://www.al-fateh.net/). Nalton et al (2011) identify a range of websites established by Dissident Irish Republicans that seem to play a similar role. They note that 'Dissident Republican propaganda material is easily available on social networking sites, and Dissident Republican web communities appear to be growing at a rate that by far outstrips the overall increase in Internet uptake in the region—even though, as noted, Northern Ireland already has the fastest growing broadband usage in the UK.'

Von Knop (2007) has suggested that young people are drawn to web-based media in three ways: accidental exposure to content while exploring the Internet for entertainment purposes; out of curiosity when seeking related information concerning ideology or traditions which may be associated with a radical group, and when looking for a social community with which they can identify. In the case of Roshonara Choudhary, it seems to have been the second of these that characterized her involvement, whereas arguably for Hammaad Munshi it was the first. Nalton et al (2011) identify examples in relation to Dissident Irish Republicans where the latter seems to be the case (i.e., looking for a social community with which they can identify).

User-generated content

The example of Hammaad Munshi raises important concerns not only about the Internet as a platform for victimization of young people but also as one which offers opportunities for young people to engage in behavior that is highly problematic. This may be the case for both sexualized and politicized behavior. In a US nationally representative survey by the Pew Research Center (Lenhart, 2009) 4% of teenagers aged 12–17 who own a mobile phone reported that they had sent sexually suggestive nude or nearly nude images of themselves to someone else via text messaging and 15% had received such images. This increases to 8% and 30% respectively in those who are 17 years old, with teenagers who pay their own bills more likely to send sexual images. This activity is frequently referred to as "sexting": the practice of sending or posting sexually suggestive text messages and images, including nude or semi-nude photographs, via cellular telephones or over the Internet (Levick & Moon, 2010). Typically, the young person takes a picture of himself or herself with a mobile phone camera (or other digital camera), or has someone else take the picture. This is then stored as a digital image and transmitted via mobile phone as a text-message, photo-send function, or electronic mail. In addition, the subject may use a mobile phone to post the image to a social networking website such as Facebook or MySpace (McBeth, 2010). Leary (2007; 2010) has referred to this material as "self-produced child pornography." Self-produced child pornography is images that possess the following criteria: they meet the legal definition of child pornography and were originally produced by a minor with no coercion, grooming, or adult participation whatsoever. The definition does not focus exclusively on the young person who makes the image but also those "juveniles in the distribution chain who may coerce production, or later possess, distribute, or utilize such images" (p 492).

Leary (2010) highlights that the term sexting has been used variously to describe a minor sending a picture to a perceived significant other; a minor taking and/or distributing pictures of himself/herself and others engaged in sexually explicit conduct; a minor extensively forwarding or disseminating a nude picture of another youth without his/her knowledge; a minor posting such pictures on a website; an older teen asking (or coercing) another youth for such pictures; a person impersonating a classmate to "dupe" and or blackmail other minors into sending pictures; and adults sending pictures or videos to minors or possessing sexually explicit pictures of juveniles and adults sending sexually suggestive text or images to other adults.

These are all different activities, only some of which would be deemed illegal in many jurisdictions (Quayle & Sinclair, in press). There is no exact equivalent of the self-production of radicalized visual material (analogous for example to sexualized images), although arguably the final "video wills" created by suicide bombers occupy such a role. On the other hand, much of the material available on sites such as IrishRepublican.net would certainly be examples of user-generated content (Nalton et al 2011).

Social networks: A broader perspective

Much of existing research on sexually abusive practices and the Internet has tended to focus on the individual, as opposed to someone within a specific social context. Yet, some of the earliest studies of this population (e.g. Durkin, 1997; Durkin & Bryant, 1999; Jenkins, 2001) related to the importance of communication with other members of online social networks. A replication of Durkin and Bryant's (1999) original study of an online "boy-lover" forum would suggest that, contrary to expectations, the use of a Usenet newsgroup as a communicative medium has not declined over a decade and that, within the forum, the use of previously identified justifications for sexual interest in children is still common (O'Halloran & Quayle, 2010). Holt, Blevins and Burkert (2010), in an analysis of postings to five "pedophile" web forums, examined their subculture and its enculturation process. The results suggested that the online world of these forum members was shaped by four interrelated normative orders—marginalization, sexuality, law, and security—which were used to generate justifications for behavior, affect attitudes toward sexual relationships with children, and structure identity. The authors suggest that this affects attitudes and beliefs, and justifies involvement in "deviance" through a rejection of larger social norms.

Seto, Reeves & Jung (2010) found that, "a substantial number of child pornography offenders, particularly in the police sample, participated in online communities and traded child pornography with others" (p 177). Similarly, in a qualitative study of a small sample of men who produced abuse images, it was found that the social function of image-taking to share with the community was the one most frequently referred to by participants (Sheehan & Sullivan, 2010).

Such research would suggest that individuals who have an interest in child pornography may receive significant reinforcement from their online relationships with others who share this interest (Taylor and Quayle, 2003). This seems also to be the case with respect to radicalization activity (Nalton et al., 2011). It also suggests that offender relationships (and associated social rewards) may be strengthened by the mutual provision of rare or personally produced images (Quayle & Taylor, 2002; Sheehan & Sullivan, 2010), a quality also illustrated by the online activity of Younis Tsouli, an important distributer of online Al Qaeda content (http://news.bbc.co.uk/1/hi/world/americas/7191248.stm).

Furthermore, individuals who engage with others using socially facilitative online applications demonstrate greater involvement in a wide range of offence-related activities than those who do not, at least with respect to sex exploitation material. It is hypothesized that, through their desire to develop and maintain online social connections, some offenders may feel compelled to produce child sexual exploitation material that they can then share with their online associates (Carr, 2009). As such, contact sex offending may result as much from a desire to please other members of an online social network as from a desire for sexual engagement with a child (Elliott & Beech, 2009). Clearly, such a finding would have significant implications for policing, offender treatment, and child protection activities (Quayle & Sinclair, in press).

One critical aspect of these social relationships may lie in Internet-initiated incitement and conspiracy to commit child sexual abuse. Gallagher (2007) presented the first research on cases where offenders initiate contact with other individuals over the Internet and incite or conspire with them to commit a contact offence. This study was an attempt to describe a typology of such offences through an examination of police data. However, the research was limited because it examined a disparate number of cases and was unable to explore the relationships between individual members, how these were formed both in the online and offline environment, how these changed over time and how they influenced others. In a further comparative study by McCarthy (2010) of "contact and non-contact child pornography offenders," contact offenders were found to be more likely than non-contact offenders to communicate both online and in person with others who shared their sexual interests in minors and abuse images. Contact offenders were also more likely to use the Internet to locate potential children and engage in grooming behavior by sending electronic files containing both child and adult pornography. There are indications that similar activities may also exist with respect to radicalization (http://news.bbc.co.uk/1/hi/world/americas/7191248.stm); it is known, for example, that some Western jihadis have been encouraged and directed to engage in jihad in Afghanistan and Somalia as a result of information and encouragement associated with Internet activity.

It would also seem to be the case that Internet-facilitated commercial sexual exploitation (IF-CSEC) has an important social element to it. Mitchell, Jones, Finkelhor, and Wolak (2011) report on telephone interviews with law enforcement related to 1,051 individual arrest cases. Of these, 569 were identified as IF-CSEC. These fell into two main categories: those who used the Internet to purchase or sell access to identified children for sexual purposes, including child pornography production (36%), and those who used the Internet to purchase or sell child pornography images they possessed but did not produce (64%). The study reported that offenders attempting to profit were more likely than those purchasing to have prior arrests for sexual and nonsexual offenses; a history of violence; produced child pornography; *joined forces with other offenders*. (The category included female offenders). These findings require further investigation. Corriveau (2010) refers to this as a subculture of deviance involving an Internet community that forms around child pornography and which helps its members to withstand the effects of external stigma while providing a framework of legitimacy over their trade.

Intervention

The report of the Homeland Security Institute (2009) asserted that efforts to counter the online radicalization of young people have thus far lagged behind terrorists' abilities to promote their messages. Interventions to date have included engagement with moderate Muslim officials to address the distorted information propagated by online forums. The report also suggests that, "For other young persons, however, for whom the terrorist appeal is 'belonging' and 'social bonding,' other approaches must be sought. The first critical step in countering youth radicalization should be to develop a better understanding, within the United States, of who our 'at risk' youth populations are and how they become susceptible to terrorist recruitment" (p 8) (see also Kessels (2010) for a discussion on the role of counter-narratives in confronting radicalization activity). This concern with "at-risk youth" echoes the one expressed by Livingstone and Brake (2010).

However, Marcum, Ricketts, and Higgins (2011) have suggested that a focus on the environment in which these crimes take place may be a more appropriate avenue. The study investigated the differences in online victimization between genders, through variables representing the three constructs of Routine Activity Theory. Cohen and Felson (1979) present a useful starting point to explore rational choice theories and Internet crime when, drawing on notions of routine activity theory, they identify three minimal elements for criminal action: a likely offender; a suitable target, and absence of a capable guardian.

Guardianship implies some form of structured and socially responsible capacity to monitor, deter, and in some sense act, if necessary. However, it does not necessarily imply government action. But given commercial realities, regardless of social outcomes in terms of effects on crime, it may well not be in a company's commercial interest to seek to adopt or develop the capable guardian role (Taylor & Quayle, 2006).

Marcum et al (2011) administered a survey to University undergraduates in the United States, which questioned respondents on their Internet behaviors and experiences during the high school senior and college freshman time period. The findings of the study indicated that participating in behaviors that increased exposure to motivated offenders and target suitability (including providing personal information to online contacts on social networking sites) in turn increased the likelihood of victimization for both genders. Conversely, taking protective measures to improve capable guardianship (such as protective software) was shown to be the least effective measure, as it did not decrease the likelihood of victimization.

We have explored the relationship between two different forms of exploitation of young people (sexual and political) through the Internet generally, and more specifically through social networking and social networking sites, suggesting that they do play a role in the engagement and exploitation of the young. Although care must be taken in exploring the parallels between these forms of exploitation, there are qualities that suggest a greater degree of commonality than might hitherto have been expected.

References

Boyd, Danah. (2007). "Why Youth (Heart) Social Network Sites: The Role of Networked Publics in Teenage Social Life." *MacArthur Foundation Series on Digital Learning – Youth, Identity, and Digital Media Volume.* (ed. David Buckingham) Cambridge, MA: MIT Press.

Briggs, P., Simon, W.T. & Simonsen, S. (2010). Internet initiated sexual offenses and the chat room sex offender: Has the Internet enabled a new typology of sex offender. *Sexual Abuse: A Journal of Research and Treatment,* 22 (4), 72–94.

Carr, A. (2009). The social dimension of the online trade of child sexual exploitation material.

Paper presented at the global symposium for examining relationship between online and offline offences and preventing the sexual exploitation of children. Chapel Hill, North Carolina, April 6–7.

Cohen, L.E., & Felson, M. (1979). Social change and crime rate trends: A routine activity approach. *American Sociological Review* 44, 588–608.

Corriveau, P. (2010). Les groups de nouvelles à caractère pédopornographique: une sous-culture de la deviance. *Déviance et Societé*, 34, 381–400.

Datan, T.D. & Mislan, R.P. (2010). Social networking: A boon to criminals. *Proceedings of the Conference on Digital Forensics, Security & Law,* p 45.

Davidson, J., Grove-Hills, J., Bifulco, A., Gottschalk, P., Caretti, V., Pham, T., Webster, S. (2011). *Online Abuse: Literature Review and Policy Context*. European Commission Safer Internet Plus Programme. Dowell, E.B., Burgess, A.W. & Cavaunaugh, D.J. (2009).Clustering of Internet risk behaviors in a middle school student population. *Journal of School Health,* 79 (11), 547–553.

Durkin, K. F. (1997). Misuse of the Internet by pedophiles: Implications for law probation practice. *Federal Probation*, 61, 14−18.

Durkin, K. F., & Bryant, C. (1999). Propagandizing pederasty: A thematic analysis of online exculpatory accounts of unrepentant paedophiles. *Deviant Behaviour: An Inter-Disciplinary Journal,* 20(2),103–127.

Elliott, I.A., & Beech, A.R. (2009). Understanding online child pornography use: Applying sexual offender theory to Internet offenders. *Aggression and Violent Behavior*, 14, 180–193.

Ellison N, Steinfield C, Lampe C. (2007). The benefits of Facebook ''friends:'' social capital and college students' use of online social network sites. *Journal of Computer-Mediated Communication,* 12: 1143–1168.

Gallagher, B. (2007) Internet-initiated incitement and conspiracy to commit child sexual abuse (CSA): The typology, extent and nature of known cases. *Journal of Sexual Aggression* 13 (2), 101–119.

Gill T. (2008). Space-oriented children's policy: creating child-friendly communities to improve children's well-being. *Children and Society* 22, 136–142.

Harris, F.J. (2010). Teens and privacy: myths and realities. *Knowledge Quest,* 39 (1), 74–79.

Holt, T.J., Blevins, K.R. & Burkert, N. (2010). Considering the pedophile culture online. *Sexual Abuse, 22 (1),* 3–24.

Homeland Security Institute. (2009). The Internet as a terrorist tool for recruitment and radicalization of youth. Arlington, VA: Homeland Security Institute.

Hoy, M.G. & Milne, G. (2010). Gender differences in privacy-related measure for young adult Facebook users. *Journal of Interactive Advertising,* 10 (2), 28–45.

Hui, J.Y. (2010). The Internet in Indonesia: Development and impact of radical websites. *Studies in Conflict and Terrorism,* 33, 171–191.

Jewkes, Y. (2010). Much ado about nothing? Representations and realities of online soliciting of children. *Journal of Sexual Aggression,* 16 (1), 5–18.

Jones, S & Fox, S. (2009). *Generations Online in 2009.* Pew Internet and American Life Project. Accessed 6 July 2010 from *http://www.pewinternet.org/~/media//Files/Reports/2009/PIP_Generations_2009.pdf.*

Kessels, E.J.A.M. (2010). *Countering Violent Extremist Narratives.* National Coordinator for Counter Terrorism, The Hague, Netherlands. Jan.

Kim, W., Jeong, O-R., Kim, C. & So, J. (2011). The dark side of the Internet: Attacks, costs and responses. *Information Systems,* 36, 75–705.

Leary, M.G. (2010). Sexting or self-produced child pornography? The dialog continues – structured prosecutorial discretion within a multidisciplinary response. *17 Va. J. Soc. Pol'y& L.* 486–566.

—. (2007) Self-produced child pornography: The appropriate societal response to juvenile self-exploitation, *15 VA. J. SOC. POL'Y & L.*1.12–14.

Lenhart. (2009). *Teens and sexting*. Pew Research Centre. Available online at *http://www.pewinternet.org/~/media//Files/Reports/2009/PIP_Teens_and_Sexting.pdf*

Levick, M. & Moon, K. (2010). Prosecuting sexting as child pornography: a critique. *44 Val. U. L. Rev*. 1035–1054.

Livingstone, S. & Brake, D.R. (2010). On the rapid rise of social networking sites: new findings and policy implications. *Children & Society,* 24, 75–83.

Livingstone, S. and Helsper, E. (2010). Balancing opportunities and risks in teenagers' use of the Internet: the role of online skills and Internet self-efficacy. *New media & society*, 12 (2). pp. 309–329.

Marcum, C.D., Ricketts, M.L. & Higgins, G.E. (2011). Assessing Sex Experiences of Online Victimization: An Examination of Adolescent Online Behaviors Utilizing Routine Activity Theory. *Deviant Behavior*, 31(5), 1–31.

Marsico, E.M. (2010). Social networking websites: Are MySpace and Facebook the fingerprints of the twenty-first century? *Weidner Law Journal,* 19, 967–976.

McBeth, I.A. (2010). Prosecute the cheerleader, save the world?: asserting federal jurisdiction over child pornography crimes committed through "sexting." *44 U. Rich. L. Rev*. 1327—1363.

Mitchell, K.J., Finkelhor, D., Jones, L.M. & Wolak, J. (2010). Use of social networking sites in online sex crimes against minors: an examination of national incidence and means of utilization. *Journal of Adolescent Health*, 47, 183–190.

Mitchell, K.J., Jones, L.M., Finkelhor, D. & Wolak, J. (2011). Internet-facilitated commercial sexual exploitation of children: Findings from a nationally representative sample of law enforcement agencies in the United States. (2010) *Sexual Abuse: A Journal of Research and Treatment*. 23 (1), 43–71.

Mitchell, K. J., Finkelhor, D., and Wolak, J. (2007). *Online requests for sexual pictures from youth: Risk factors and incident characteristics. Journal of Adolescent Health*, 41, 196–203.

Nalton, J, Ramsey, G., and Taylor, M. (2011). Radicalisation and Internet propaganda by Dissident Republican Groups in Northern Ireland since 2008. In *Dissident Irish Republicanism*. Currie, P.M. and Taylor, M. New York: Continuum Press.

O'Halloran, E., & Quayle, E. (2010). A content analysis of a "boy-love" support forum: Revisiting Durkin and Bryant. *Journal of Sexual Aggression*, 16, 71–85. Quayle, E. & Sinclair, R. (in press).

Quayle, E and Taylor, M. (2002). Child pornography and the Internet: Perpetuating a cycle of abuse. *Deviant Behavior,* 23 (4), 331–362.

Regan, P. & Steeves, V. (2010). Kids R US: Online social networking and the potential for empowerment. *Surveillance and Society*, 8 (2), 151–165.

Seto, M. C., Reeves, L., & Jung, S. (2010). Motives for child pornography offending: The explanations given by the offenders. *Journal of Sexual Aggression,* 16, 169–180.

Sharples, M., Graber, R., Harrison, C. & Logan, K. (2010). E-Safety on Web 2.0 for children aged 11–16. *Journal of Computer Assisted Learning,* 25, 70–84.

Sheehan, V. & Sullivan, J. (2010). A qualitative analysis of child sex offenders involved in the manufacture of indecent images of children. *Journal of Sexual Aggression,* 16 (2), 143–168.

Taraszow, T., Aristodemou, E., Shitta, G., Laouris, Y. & Arsoy, A. (2010). Disclosure of personal and contact information by young people in social networking sites: An analysis using Facebook profiles as an example. *International Journal of Media and Cultural Politics,* 6 (1), 81–102.

Taylor, M. and Quayle, E. (2006). The Internet and abuse images of children; search, pre-criminal situations and opportunity. In Wortley, R. and Smallbone, S. (Eds) "*Situational perspectives of Sexual Offences against Children*" Crime Prevention Studies Series (jointly published by Criminal Justice Press (US) and Willan Publishing (UK).

Taylor, M. & Ramsay, G. (2010). Violent Radical Content and the Relationship between Ideology and Behaviour: Do Counter-Narratives Matter? In National Coordinator for Counter Terrorism, *Countering Violent Extremist Narratives*. The Hague: Netherlands.

Taylor, M & Quayle, E. (2003). *Child Pornography: An Internet Crime.* Brighton: Routledge.

The Daily Telegraph, 30 May, 2014. Terrorism and child pornography used to justify surveillance society, says academic. Accessed online 3 June from *http://www.telegraph.co.uk/technology/news/7054432/Terrorism-and-child-pornography-used-to-justify-surveillance-society-says-academic.html*

The Mail Online, 19 August, 2008. Guilty: Britain's youngest ever terrorist, 16, who had guide to death and explosives in his home. Accessed online 12, December 2009 from *http://www.dailymail.co.uk/news/article-1046472/Guilty-Britains-youngest-terrorist-16-guide-death-explosives-home.html*

The Times, October 17, 2008. Link between child porn and Muslim terrorists discovered in police raids. Accessed online 11 February 2009 from http://www.timesonline.co.uk/tol/news/uk/crime/article4959002.ece.

Tufekci, Zeynep (2008), "Can You See Me Now? Audience and disclosure regulation in online social network sites," *Bulletin of Science, Technology & Society,* 28 (1), 20-36.

UNODC (2010) Vienna: United Nations Office on Drugs and Crime.

Valkenburg P M, & Peter J. (2007). Internet communication and its relation to well-being: identifying some underlying mechanisms. *Media Psychology* 9, 43–58.

Van Manen, M. (2010). The pedagogy of Momus technologies: Facebook, privacy and online intimacy. *Qualitative Health Research,* 20 (8), 1023–1032.

Weimann, G. (2010). Terror on Facebook, Twitter and YouTube. *Brown Journal of World Affairs,* 16 (2), 45–54.

Wolak, J., Finkelhor D. & Mitchell, K. (2009). *Trends in arrests of "online predators."* University of New Hampshire: Crimes against Children Research Centre.

Wolak, J., Finkelhor, D., Mitchell, K., and Ybarra, M. (2008). *Online "Predators" and Their Victims: Myths, Realities, and Implications for Prevention and Treatment.* **American Psychologist**, 63(2), 111–128.

Ybarra, M., Mitchell, K., Finkelhor, D., and Wolak, J. (2007). *Internet prevention messages: Targeting the right online behaviors.* ***Archives of Pediatrics & Adolescent Medicine, 161:*** 138–145.

CHAPTER SIX

EDUCATION FOR ADULT PARENTING

JOHN SHEA

Introduction

Why is it important to talk about *adult* parenting? What does being an adult add to what it means to be a parent? Do parents need to be adults in our contemporary culture, and, if so, why is that important? And if it is important that parents be adults, what needs to be considered in adult parenting education?

Reflections on contemporary culture

There are a number of observations about the kind of culture that most families find themselves in that make the notion of adult parenting not only helpful for raising children in the world of today but also make this notion necessary in ways that perhaps just forty or fifty years ago would have been much harder to understand.

1. Today, ***roles of parents are not as easily defined as in the past.*** Both parents were, of course, always important in the raising of their children, but the roles of women and men in many parts of the world are changing quite dramatically. The consciousness of women's equality in particular has made a significant difference in the ways women are understood in society and in the ways women understand themselves. These understandings are not only reflected in how parenting roles are being redefined but also in how educational needs and financial concerns are assessed in the family.
2. Today, ***the family is under pressure and in transition.*** Captured and tossed by changing economies and differing ideologies, the family is alternately a joy, a liability, the "first teacher," a regressive institution, a financial unit, a political football, and a sacred entity. From being

assumed to be the natural foundation of society, the family is becoming a social and economic reality to be dealt with in an increasingly complex, competitive, and commoditized world. Today, what "family" means is at play in what "human development" means, in what "the good life" is supposed to be, and in how notions of "wealth" and "commonwealth" are weighed together.

3. Today, ***many social institutions are not particularly supportive of the family.*** As the needs of families increase and become more complex, and at the same time, as globalization spurs economic competition, as the commodification of the person takes greater hold, as standards of living are rising, as notions of "normalcy" and "success" are more influenced by purchasing power and consumption of goods, many of the institutions that serve the family—especially educational and healthcare institutions—are in transition. They are often not sufficiently resourced and not able to adequately service the many needs of families.
4. Today, ***culture no longer clearly tells us how we should act.*** In the past, tradition and what we might call "the cultural superego" had a great deal of influence on the family and on all roles in society. There were accepted ways of being and doing. Now, with mass communication and especially with television and the Internet, culture speaks with many voices, telling us there are many ways to be. Now it is up to us to consciously choose the ways that are best. If in the past there was a sense that values were fixed and handed down, now with "the decline of tradition" there are "increasing pressures to choose one's own form of life autonomously" (Kleingeld, 2004, p. 32).
5. Today, ***the authority of many religious institutions has been eroded.*** On the one hand, the cultural changes we are naming have an effect on the acceptance of religious teachings and values. On the other hand, many religious institutions themselves seem to be losing their authority because of poor leadership, too much corruption and scandal, too much authoritarianism, and too much insensitivity to the deeper aspirations of their congregants. As a reflection of these problems, "religion" is increasingly defined in culture as being about dogmas, creeds, and rituals, while "spirituality" is seen as personally chosen, animating, trustworthy, and meaningful.

In the light of these and many other changes that have occurred culturally in the past fifty years, it is clear—for good or for ill—that the family is no longer carried by "the cultural superego," that defined roles are in flux, that authorities speak less powerfully, that inequality is understood for the personal and social injustice that it is, and that institutions are less able to care for the expanding needs of the family. If the culture cannot support the family as it once did, and if family relationships are themselves being redefined, then parents who are adults are more and more important in the raising of their children. It was always true that "it takes an adult to raise a child," but now this dictum has a deeper meaning that we cannot afford to ignore.

Adult Self, Adult Parent

What is an adult self? An adult self is a self that has grown up and come into its own possession. As we become adult, our locus of valuing moves from others outside of us to a place within the self. As adults we are our own coherent, self-authoring whole. An adult self is, therefore, its own whole, a whole that functions from within. This whole or integral self is not, of course, a perfect whole without blind spots and shortcomings, but it is a whole that is coherent enough to function from within itself with a comfortable sense of confidence and agency.

Functioning as its own whole, an adult self relates to whomever or whatever is other—husband or wife, children, friends, the disadvantaged, and even events and institutions—in a way that respects who or what that other is in its uniqueness. When we are adults, we relate to the other, no matter who or what that other is, with genuine concern for the other's particular character and developmental needs. In other words, if we are adults, we relate to whomever or whatever is other in *considered mutuality*. Like integrity, this relating in considered mutuality is essential to being a mature adult, and like integrity, relating in mutuality is often imperfect and somewhat ragged at the edges. Still, *an adult self is an integral self—relating to the other in considered mutuality*. And, of course, an adult parent is defined in exactly the same way.

Integrity

What is the integrity that along with mutuality characterizes an adult self and an adult parent? There are many ways of defining integrity. For many, integrity means honesty, or fairness, or "lying neither about nor to oneself" (Parizeau, 1999, p. 164). An excellent definition of integrity is offered by Robert Grudin (1990) in *The Grace of Great Things*:

"Integrity is
1. an inner psychological harmony, or wholeness;
2. a conformity of personal expression with psychological reality—of act with desire, of word with thought, of face with mind, of the outer with the inner self; and;
3. an extension of wholeness and conformity in time, through thick and thin. Though integrity can be, and must be, expressed in individual actions, it is not fully realized except in terms of continuity" (p. 74).

Grudin concludes this definition by saying: "Thus understood, integrity may be defined as psychological and ethical wholeness, sustained in time."[4]

We can briefly reflect on Grudin's understanding of integrity in the light of adult parenting:

1. To define integrity as "an inner psychological harmony, or wholeness" is to capture its main meaning. A whole self is a self in which all its inner "pieces"—whether thought of as aspects, or elements, or parts—function together. A whole self is not made up of pieces that remain disconnected, or isolated, or disowned. All the pieces—however different or difficult they may be—must be intimately connected. They come together in a way that allows them to function as a whole. If parents have not yet become this kind of whole person, the "pieces" that are not integrated in them tend to be visited on their children. A mother or father's fear, or trauma, or insecurity, or self-centeredness, or unresolved anger can easily become the child's fear, or insecurity, or anger. The problem we have as parents, says Robert Karen (1998), is usually "not lack of love or good intentions" but "an unwillingness to *face who we are*" (p. 378). A father or a mother who is not enough of his or her own whole tends not to understand all the "pieces" that the child needs to become his or her own whole.
2. To see integrity as "conformity of the outer with the inner self" is a secondary characteristic of integrity, yet this definition of integrity is probably the one we think of first. For a person to have integrity, the "outer" must be in harmony with the "inner." In judging character—our own or another's—we look for honesty, truthfulness, sincerity, and authenticity. Children are often incredibly adept in judging the integrity of others—especially their parents—in those matters that they can relate to. As they are growing up, children have to struggle with honesty, truthfulness, sincerity, and authenticity. They have an innate sensitivity to issues of integrity, and they are constantly looking to their parents to see if lying, stealing, and cheating are acceptable.

As popular wisdom attests, it is not what the parents say that is most important but rather what the parents do. "Children feel the conflicts and contradictions that parents bring to the dynamics of family life. They quickly recognize when there is a dissonance between what parents demand and expect of them and the value by which their parents live" (Gordon, 2005, p. 115). Influenced as they are by others and by the culture, children have a great need for parents who have integrity. They need to learn that a person with integrity "respects the rights of others, even (in extreme cases) to his or her own detriment or risk" (Rayner, (1999, p. 193).

3. To see integrity as "an extension of wholeness and conformity in time, through thick and thin" and to see that "it is not fully realized except in terms of continuity" completes its definition. The integrity that characterizes adulthood and adult parenting is only proved over time. It is over time, then, that all the different "pieces" of the self must be owned and kept connected. It is over time that the "outer" must be in harmony with the "inner." The challenge of integrity over time is to "stand for something and remain steadfast when confronted with adversity or temptation" (Paine, 2005, p. 248). "Acting morally," says Gil Noam (1993), "involves taking a stand, often an unpopular one" (p. 219).

In a culture where there are so many pressures and so many contradictory values at play, it may take a great deal of courage for parents to hold on to their integrity. "Parents are called to be courageously steadfast in living and sharing their own values and wisdom if they are to demonstrate the importance of overcoming the empty mind-set of consumerism and immediate gratification" (Carey, 2003, p. 102). As Seamus Carey observes, "courage is perhaps the virtue most called on in parenting" (p. 100). Still, a courageous, sustained integrity is not easy to come by. "Integrity," says John Beebe (1992), "cannot survive without an attitude of vigilance, and we are always, in effect, restoring our integrity from some attempt at compromise" (p. 40).

Mutuality

In "Naturalistic Conceptions of Moral Maturity," Lawrence Walker and Russell Pitts (1998) found two overall characteristics of the moral person. On the one hand, "the highly moral person has a range of strongly held values and principles" that are "joined by a strong sense of self and personal agency." On the other hand, this is coupled with "notions of communion" and "by an other-oriented compassion and care that entails helpful, thoughtful and considerate action and the nurturing of relationships thorough faithfulness and reliability (pp. 414-415). Walker and Pitts are saying in different words that integrity goes hand in hand with mutuality. So the question for us is: What is the mutuality that along with integrity characterizes an adult self and an adult parent? If a clearly nuanced definition of integrity is critical for understanding adulthood and adult parenting, a clearly nuanced definition of relating in mutuality is critical as well.

Four aspects of what it means for adults to relate in considered mutuality are considered here:

1. *Relating in mutuality takes the other just as the other is in its uniqueness.* This is, as we have seen, the hallmark of relating in mutuality. From the very beginning of life, "mutuality enables the self to be what it is and become what it is becoming" (Willeford, 1987, p. 145). As we relate to the becoming self, there is no such thing as a "generalized other." There are only actual others with specific needs, aspirations, and backgrounds. "Crucial to a mature sense of mutuality," observes Judith Jordan (1991), "is an appreciation of the wholeness of the other person, with a special awareness of the other's subjective experience" (p. 82). In relating in mutuality in marriage, "it is of the utmost importance to be sensitive to the uniqueness of one's spouse and the details of the relationship" (Kleingeld, 2004, p. 36). In relating in mutuality to our children, the distinctness of each child is recognized, along with that child's needs and the particular concerns. In this relating, each child can grow as his or her unique self. "Good parenting," as Mufid Hannush (2002) observes, "makes it possible (enables) children to become their true selves, to develop a good character" (p. 8). "When each individual within the family is regarded as unique and worthy of respect, family members flourish" (Anderson et al., 2004, p. 1).
2. *Relating in mutuality is love and care for the integrity of the other.* "Becoming accomplished in the mutuality of love "is the indispensable key to becoming human" (Wadel, 2004, p. 12). And what is love? "Love is the thoughtful and deliberate practice of attending to the needs, concerns, and well-being of others" (p. 14). All of us—and especially our children —are in need of this kind of love flowing from integrity. This kind of love is "essential for moral development and personality integration" (Hannush, 2002, p. 2). It is love and care, especially in the early years of life, that allow for gradual growth in human and moral maturity. "Parents are children's most important

teachers. It is the experience of the early years, mediated by parenting, which sets the child on a trajectory of either success or failure. A child's confidence, her concept of self, her readiness to launch herself into fearless learning and healthy relationships, are dependent on and intricately bound up in the quality of nurturing she receives from a loving adult" (Gordon, 2005, p. 17).

Erik Erikson's (1964) notion of loving care has an ethic of mutuality built into it. "*Care is the widening concern for what has been generated by love, necessity, or accident; it overcomes the ambivalence adhering to irreversible obligation*" (p. 131). In other words, an adult parent loves and cares simply because there is a child who needs love and care. This caring *is* mutuality as Erikson sees it, because it forms "a relationship in which partners depend on each other for the development of their respective strengths" (p. 231). This kind of mutuality is operating in relationships throughout the cycle of life. The care that the adult parent *needs to offer* is the care that the child *needs to receive*. Caring "*strengthens the doer even as it strengthens the other*" (p. 233). In caring, both the parent and the child are able to grow and further their own wholeness. The fullness of life revolves around adult caring.

3. *Relating in mutuality insists on justice for the other*. Susan Ross (1995) points out that that the notion of mutuality suggests "the principles of responsiveness and justice in relationship" (p. 55). This understanding of mutuality, vital as it is in the life of the family, must first be found in the relation between husband and wife. In many marriages, however, there is often a problem. "According to the current normative ideal of marriage," says Pauline Kleingeld (2004), "principles of justice that we generally recognize as holding between individuals are actually *suspended* within marriage, because 'normal' marriage partners are thought to interact exclusively on the basis of care and affection" (p. 25). In other words, the spousal relationship is seen as a matter of love and not of justice. "Marriage as a social institution," says Kleingeld, "is still largely determined by gender ideology as well as by laws, policies, and institutions that reinforce the traditional patriarchal form of marriage" (p. 25).

   Relating in mutuality is not applying abstract principles of justice to others as if everyone were the same; it is understanding that only if the particularities of each party are known can justice be realized. "Unless one defends a notion of justice as a mathematically even distribution of goods regardless of the needs and desires of the individuals in question, the very specific personality traits, desires, needs and values of both spouses are crucial in their attempt to find out what is just" (Kleingeld, 2004, p. 26). If the parents are the child's "first teachers," and if marriage as a social institution is still governed by patriarchal norms, the kind of mutuality that fosters interpersonal justice cannot be learned by our children. If family life is conceived of as a matter of love and not of justice, then our children will learn that human desires, needs, and values need not be seen in a way that love and justice go together. But mutuality is not about love *or* justice; mutuality is about love *and* justice, taking into account "the unique details of the relationship." "A great deal of our integrity," says Jack Dominian (1985), "relies on how well we can listen to others, for an accurate and sensitive interpretation of what they are saying is due to them in justice and love" (p. 37).

4. *Relating in mutuality does not demand relating in mutuality in return.* Adult parenting is parenting done by an adult self, a felt-from-within whole, who relates to spouse, children, and anything else that is other in considered mutuality. *It is our own wholeness that finds the wholeness of the other.* This is the wonderful thing about being an adult, and this is why being an adult is so important for understanding moral development and for understanding good parenting. As adults, we come to be responsible for our own wholeness. Growing up, we need the integrity of adults to help us to realize that wholeness, but as mature adults we are able to relate in mutuality whether or not others are able to respond in kind. Integrity and relating in considered mutuality are a wonderful gift and invitation. "Children naturally imitate and identify with parents who consistently care for and love them" (Hannush, 2002, p. 3). However, this gift and this invitation to wholeness and mutuality are not—and can never be—a contract or a reciprocal agreement.

If we have sufficient power or authority, we can make demands on our children that produce conformity, but we cannot make them be something "inside" that they are not. Rules have their place in any family and any well-functioning society, but obedience to the rule is not enough for authentic morality. Being adult and being authentically moral must come from "inside." It is considered mutuality—it is love, justice, and honoring uniqueness—that nourishes a child, giving sustenance and strength and eventually allowing the "felt-from-within" to respond. If there is any calculus for adult parenting, that calculus is love and justice and honoring the unique needs and concerns of all in the family.

Empathy and care for the other

If integrity with considered mutuality allows us, in love and justice, to pay attention to the needs, concerns, and values of the other, we need to ask: "How does that happen? How are we able to know what the 'inside' of the other is like? How can we be sensitive to the particular concerns of the other? How can we know the uniqueness of the other?" The best answer to these questions is rather clear, if not immediately obvious: "We need to relate to the other in *empathy*." It is empathy that lets us know what the "inside" of the other is like. It is empathy that reveals to us the particular concerns and uniqueness of the other. And, as we will see, it is empathy that is at the heart of adulthood and adult parenting.

But what is empathy? "Empathy," according to Ralph Greenson (1967), "means to share, to experience the feelings of another human being" (p. 368). Heinz Kohut (1984), sees empathy as "the capacity to think and feel oneself into the inner life of another person" (p. 82). Carl Rogers (1959), in what has become a classical definition, says: "The state of empathy, or being empathic, is to perceive the internal frame of reference of another with accuracy and with the emotional components and meanings which pertain thereto, as if one were the other person, but without ever losing the 'as if' condition" (p. 210).

My working definition is: empathy is one person feeling—with an attitude of care and concern—what the other person feels, as if one were the other person (but knowing one is not); it involves sensing the emotions, the attitudes, the way of seeing things, the way of relating, and the meanings the other person senses.

Five things are very important to point out immediately about the *nature* of empathy, because even though empathy is such a foundational human ability, it is still easily misunderstood. First, the "feeling" talked about is not just emotion, but it is a *felt sensing*; it is, as Rogers (1959) says, "an emotionally tinged experience together with its personal meaning" (p. 198). In other words, the "feeling" that empathy is trying to grasp has both *cognition* and *emotion* within it; in "feeling" the whole person, the *mind* and the *body*, are revealed together. Second, empathy is a *paradox*; one has to feel what the other feels as if one were the other person, and at the same time one has to remain distinctly separate from the other person. Third, the attitude of *care and concern* is essential to empathy; as Edward Farley (1996) notes: "Empathy not only feels with another but would cease the other's suffering and promote the other's well-being" (p. 296). Fourth, to have empathy for the other *does not mean that you agree* with the other; it simply means that you are able to sense how the other person is feeling "inside." Fifth, although some people seem to think that empathy is quite unusual, it is actually a skill that touches the very depth of our humanness and that is quite capable of being developed.

Five things that Rogers (1980) describes about the actual *practice* of empathy are helpful to get a sense of what it is like to be empathic. First, empathy means "entering the private perceptual world of the other and becoming thoroughly at home in it" so that you are "a confident companion to the person in his or her inner world" (p. 142). Second, empathy "involves being sensitive, moment by moment, to the changing felt meanings which flow in this other person, to the fear or rage or tenderness or confusion or whatever that he or she is experiencing" (p. 142). Third, empathy "means temporarily living in the other's life, moving about in it delicately without making judgments" (p. 142). Fourth, empathy "includes communicating your sensings of the person's world as you look with fresh and unfrightened eyes at elements of which he or she is fearful" (p. 142). Fifth, empathy "means frequently checking with the person as to the accuracy of your sensings, and being guided by the responses you receive" (p. 142). Rogers is talking about empathy the way a therapist might actively embody this "way of being" with a client, but anyone who embodies this wonderful personal skill will help the other person to feel more whole, to feel better understood, and to be better able to move forward in a positive direction. Empathy touches the "inside" of the other and the "inside" of the self in a way that nothing else can, and it changes both.

Empathy, adulthood, and parenting education

As we bring empathy, adulthood, and parenting education together, the most important thing to say is that being an adult and having empathy naturally go together. Empathic knowing is at the heart of integrity because it is empathy for ourselves that lets us own all of our "pieces," the good, the bad and the ugly; empathy with ourselves lets us know everything that we are feeling about ourselves, and this allows us to feel and be whole. As we have seen, empathic knowing is at the heart of mutuality; empathy lets us be with the "feeling" of the other, allowing us to understand the particular needs and the unique perspectives of the other, allowing the other to understand herself or himself better and to feel and be more whole. Even more, empathic knowing makes a unique *bond* between me and the other, allowing each of us to feel and be more ourselves and more connected (see Jordan, 1997). That empathy, then, should be so important in how parents relate to each other and to their children is no surprise. Writing about family violence and nurturing parenting, Stephen Bavolek (2000) observes: "The effect of inadequate empathic parental care during the early years of life is profound and enduring" (p. 4). He goes on to attest: "Empathy is the single most desirable quality in nurturing parenting" (p. 5).

The question now is: can we approach parenting education in a way that adult empathy is central to it? And if we can, what will allow this to happen? Well, there is a way to make adult empathy central in parenting education, and for this to happen, three things need to be in place in parenting education programmes: (1) those who are running adult parenting education programs must be reasonably coherent adult selves, capable of fostering empathy in the participants; (2) those who are running adult parenting education programs must have sufficient knowledge and expertise about parenting issues and skills; and (3) those who are running adult parenting education programs must have some vision of what adult parenting is. Let us look at these three elements in turn:

(1) *Those who are running adult parenting education programmes must be reasonably coherent adult selves, capable of fostering empathy in the participants.* It is easy to see how important it is to have adults running the program who can be empathic to the parents and the children who come to the program. Parenting can be extremely challenging and frustrating for all involved, and to have someone knowledgeable who has genuine empathy with what the participants are going through can be very validating and very freeing. If the adults who are running the program are empathic, it is easier for the participants in the program—parents and children as well—to develop empathy themselves. Empathy, like antipathy, is contagious. Should the participants have feelings of rage, shame, inadequacy, helplessness, and desperately needing to control, these feelings can be mitigated all around.

A second reason why it is so important to have empathic adults running parenting programs is developmental. Robert Selman (1980), a thinker in the tradition of Jean Piaget, has a "level" theory of perspective taking that in some ways is similar to the development of empathy. With a lot of adaptation, his description of Level 2: "Reciprocal Perspective Taking" is, I believe, a good description of how parents who are not yet adult tend to relate to each other and to their children. With a lot of adaptation, his Level 3: "Mutual Perspective Taking" has, I believe, the beginnings of adult relating in empathy. Parts of his description of these two levels are helpful for us to see how the ability to be empathic might develop in a parenting education program.

In Level 2, "Reciprocal Perspective Taking," I know what I think and feel and I also know what you think and feel. If you are in this level of perspective taking, you know the same about me. There is "a two-way reciprocity." I can put myself in your shoes and you can put yourself in my shoes. At this stage, social cognition is: "I know that she knows that I know she knows" (p. 38). There is some degree of empathy for the "inner feelings" of the other, but the limitation of this level is that although I can know my own perspective and I can know your perspective in a rudimentary way, I cannot see the systems of relationship we are both part of. In other words, I am "locked into" my relationship with you. I cannot yet *stand outside* of our relationship to *get unenmeshed* in it, to *get distance from* it, to *look at* it, to *evaluate* it, to *understand* it. Many parents, it seems, have this kind of reciprocal relationship with each other and with their children; they are "locked into" a back-and-forth exchange with the other that does not have a lot of understanding and that can easily escalate into shouting, blaming, fighting, and different ways of hurting the other and "getting back at the other."

In Level 3, "Mutual Perspective Taking," I can step outside of the different relationships that I am in to *look at* myself and to *look at* you, and especially to *reflect on* the relationship itself. At this stage, I develop an "observing ego." I can take a "third-person perspective" on what is going on in my relationships and reflect on them as if I were another person. For example, I can *step back* from the situation, *reflect* on it, and *talk to myself*. I might say to myself:

> Well, this is interesting. We are having the same fight again, the one we almost always have. What is going on here? Is it something about me? Is it something about her? Is it the situation we are in? What triggers this? And how does our son figure in all of this? Why does our son always get me so angry? He pushes all my buttons. Is it because he is so much like me? Is his mother protecting him too much? Why would she be doing that? Let me *get some distance* and *think about* all this so I can *see* more clearly what is going on. What are all the pieces that are a part of this whole scene? What is really happening? What can I do differently?

This mutual way of relating has more empathy in it. I am more whole, more myself, and I can see the others' perspectives with more nuance and more interconnection. Because I am enough of a whole person, I can relate more in mutuality. Comfortable enough as who I am, I can *stand outside* of myself and *see* my needs and values and those of others in context. I can *see* the whole situation with an "observing ego" and perhaps respond appropriately. Level 3 speaks to an advance in empathy that can make a major difference in the lives of parents and children. If adults are running the parenting program, and if perhaps there are some adults who are participants, then there is an atmosphere of empathy and self-reflection that can help those parents who are at Level 2 to move toward Level 3. In other words, an adult parenting program is able to foster the quality of empathy that makes for adult parenting.

(2) *Those running adult parenting education programmes must have sufficient knowledge and expertise about parenting issues and skills.* There are many different kinds of parenting education programs, all based on knowledge and expertise about parenting, and all concerned with teaching healthy ways to nurture children. We mention five programs here to suggest some of the possibilities, paying special attention to how these programs are able to foster empathy.

1. *Mentoring Parent Programs.* These programs usually "teach by telling" as a way of mentoring parents in their interactions with their children, but they also try to provide insight into problems and issues that parents are concerned about. Mentors with empathy can relate mutually with the parents who come to this kind of program, allaying shame and embarrassment and allowing the parents to become more empowered in their parenting.
2. *Filial Therapy Programs*: "Typically, filial therapy takes place in a support-group format in which the parents learn basic child-centred play therapy principles and skills to utilize with their children in special weekly play sessions" (Bratton & Landreth, 1995, p. 62). Play therapy can be an excellent way of having empathy for what the child is experiencing as well as an excellent way for the child to reveal what is "inside."
3. *Sympathetic Coaching Programs*: A trained coach works with a group of parents with their children on more positive ways of relating to how the child is acting. These programs might be better named "empathic coaching" because the goal here is not to feel "for" the child from the outside, but to feel "with" the child "inside" and respond appropriately.
4. *Role-playing Programs:* In these groups, the parent may take the role of the child or experiment with some new way of communicating with his or her child. These programs are wonderful for experiencing empathy because they connect the "inside" of the parent with the "inside" of the child.

5. *Parent Discussion Programs:* In these programs, parents get together and share what they are experiencing in raising their children. Different perspectives on child rearing come from the members of the group. If an atmosphere of mutuality can be honored in the group, empathy and support for all involved are easily able to surface.

(3) *Those running adult parenting education programs must have some vision of what adult parenting is.* In "Parenting across the Lifespan," Martin Herbert (2004) offers some guidelines for parenting that are a practical way to conclude this presentation. These guidelines not only capture a lot of the hard-earned wisdom that animates adult parenting education programs but are also substantially in harmony with the vision of adult parenting presented here:

Guideline 1: Foster Bonds of respect and affection.
Guideline 2: Make firm social and moral demands (set limits).
Guideline 3: Prepare children for life by developing family routines.
Guideline 4: Teach children the family rules.
Guideline 5: Choose rules carefully.
Guideline 6: Be consistent.
Guideline 7: Be persistent.
Guideline 8: Give explanations/reasons.
Guideline 9: Tell children what they should do, not only what they should not do.
Guideline 10: Give responsibility.
Guideline 11: Listen careful to what the child says (pp. 68-69).

Carey (2003) makes a point about this last guideline that throws a nice reflective light on how integrity and mutuality go together in adult parenting: "Empathic connections with others, including our children, do not preclude strong and decisive decision making and leadership. In fact, the insights that skilful listening and hearkening provide are a prerequisite for the strongest and most convincing leadership a parent can offer" (p. 78).

References

Anderson, H., Foley, E., Miller-McLemore, B., & Schreiter, R. (2004). Introduction. In H. Anderson, E. Foley, B. Miller-McLemore & R. Schreiter (Eds.), *Mutuality matters: Family, faith, and just love* (pp 1-8). Lanham, MD: Rowman & Littlefield.

Bavolek, S. (2000). The nurturing parenting programs. *Juvenile Justice Bulletin*, November, 1-13.

Beebe, J. (1992). *Integrity in depth*. College Station, TX: Texas A&M University Press.

Bratton, S. & Landreth, G. (1995). Filial therapy with single parents: Effects on parental acceptance, empathy, and stress. *International Journal of Play Therapy, 4*(1), 61-80.

Carey, S. (2003). *The whole child: Restoring wonder to the art of parenting*. New York: Rowman & Littlefield.

Dominian, J. (1985). *The capacity to love*. London: Darton Longman & Todd.

Erikson, E. (1964). *Insight and responsibility: Lectures on the ethical implications of psychoanalytic insight*. New York: Norton.

Farley, E. (1996). *Divine empathy: A theology of god*. Minneapolis, MN: Fortress.

Gordon, M. (2005). *Roots of empathy: Changing the world child by child*. Toronto: Thomas Allen.

Greenson, R. R. (1967). *The technique and practice of psychoanalysis, Volume l*. New York: International Universities Press.

Grudin, R. (1990). *The grace of great things: Creativity and Innovation*. New York: Ticknor & Fields.

Hannush, M. J. (2002). *Becoming good parents: An existential journey*. Albany, NY: State University of New York Press.

Herbert, M. (2004). Parenting across the lifespan. In M. Hoghughi & N. Long (Eds.), *Handbook of parenting: Theory and research for practice* (pp. 55-71). New Delhi: Sage.

Jordan, J. V. (1991). The meaning of mutuality. In J. V. Jordan, A. G. Kaplan, J. B. Miller, I. P. Stiver, & J. L. Surrey (Eds.), *Women's growth in connection: Writings from the Stone* center (pp. 81-96). New York: Guilford Press.

Jordan, J. V. (1997). Relational development through mutual empathy. In A. C. Bohart & and L. S. Greenberg (Eds.), *Empathy reconsidered: New directions in psychotherapy* (pp. 343-351). Washington, DC: American Psychological Association.

Karen, R. (1998). *Becoming attached: First relationships and how they shape our capacity to love*. New York: Oxford University Press.

Kleingeld, P. (2004). Just love? Marriage and the question of justice. In H. Anderson, E. Foley, B. Miller-McLemore & R. Schreiter (Eds.), *Mutuality matters: Family, faith, and just love* (pp 23-41). Lanham, MD: Rowman & Littlefield.

Kohut, H. (1984). *How does analysis cure?* Chicago: University of Chicago Press.

Noam, G. G. (1993). 'Normative vulnerabilities' of self and their transformations in moral action. In G. G. Noam & T. E. Wren (Eds.), *The moral self* (pp. 209-238).Cambridge, MA: MIT Press.

Paine, L. S. (2005). Integrity. In P. H. Werhane & R. E. Freeman (Eds.), *The Blackwell encyclopedia of management: Business ethics*, 2nd ed. (pp. 247-249). Malden, MA: Blackwell.

Parizeau, M-H. (1999). Scientific integrity. In A. Montefiore & D. Vines (Eds.), *Integrity in the public and private domains* (pp. 152-165). London: Routledge.

Rayner, C. (1999). Integrity in surgical life: What happens if it is missing? In A. Montefiore & D. Vines (Eds.), *Integrity in the public and private domains* (pp. 179-188). London: Routledge.

Rogers, C. R. (1959). A theory of therapy, personality, and interpersonal relationships, as developed in the client-centered framework. In S. Koch (Ed.), *Psychology: A study of a science* (Vol. 3, pp. 184-256). New York: McGraw-Hill.

Rogers, C. R. (1980). Empathic: An unappreciated way of being. In *A way of being* (pp. 137-163). Boston: Houghton Mifflin.

Ross, S. A. (1995). Evil and hope: Foundational Moral Perspectives. In P. Crowley (Ed.), *Proceedings of the Catholic Theological Society of America* (pp. 46-62). Santa Clara, CA: University of Santa Clara Press.

Selman, R. L. (1980). *The growth of interpersonal understanding: Developmental and clinical analyses.* New York: Academic Press.

Wadel, P. J. (2004). The family as a crucible of grace: Finding god in the mutuality of love. In H. Anderson, E. Foley, B. Miller-McLemore & R. Schreiter (Eds.), *Mutuality matters: Family, faith, and just love* (pp 11-21). Lanham, MD: Rowman & Littlefield.

Walker, L. J. & Pitts, R. C. (1998). Naturalistic conceptions of moral maturity. *Developmental Psychology 34*(3), 403-419.

Willeford, W. (1987). *Feeling, imagination, and the self: Transformations of the mother-infant relationship.* Evanston, IL: Northwestern University Press.

CHAPTER SEVEN

GLOBALIZATION AND CHILDREN

M K. GEORGE

Introduction

> *"Boy and Girl prostitutes in Thailand hired by French tourists; child pornography on the Internet; five-year old indentured textile workers in India making silk for American clothing; Eastern European adolescent girls assaulted and raped as they seek glamorous careers on Milan's runways…startling images that confront us regularly as the economy becomes a global network and as our means to communicate information penetrates into and out of every village and hamlet…As our planet shrinks in size will we sacrifice children to the yawning and ever more visible gulf between the richest and poorest nations of the earth?"* (Fass, 2003:1)

Globalization is not only reshaping the political economy of the world, it is also reshaping families and definitely the future of children. So the enquiry of how globalization influences children becomes a crucial one. In spite of many and varied attempts, globalization often defies precise definition. In fact, there has even been a sense of cynicism in the way globalization has been used as a "cheap flavor enhancer" (Rizzini and Bush, 2002). However, the various definitions, when they are used as explanatory principles and as a way of comprehending the enormous changes produced in the world, do help us comprehend the phenomenon and enter into discourses, leading to creative responses to the new reality that the intensified globalization processes have initiated during the last couple of decades.

In this discussion on globalization and children, we look at globalization primarily in terms of its economic and cultural impacts. It is not to claim that the other dimensions, particularly the political one, are not important. In many cases, the political impact of the globalization processes, with the neo-colonial forces that are operative behind the scenes, may be more important in comprehending the world reality. We look at the major economic and cultural impacts of globalization and its corresponding significance for the children of the world.

A conceptual model

The field of discourse on globalization and children is so vast that some sort of conceptual model would be essential to understand the process. I would like to adapt a model which was initially used by UNICEF to study the impact of World Recession on Children (1984). It gives us a hint of the broad framework within which this reality could be looked at.

Factors that bring about changes in the welfare of children are as follows:

1. Family and Community circumstances
2. Household income
3. Government expenditure.

The following class of indicators will measure the consequences due to changes in the above areas:

i. Input Indicators
   a. Unemployment rates
   b. Real household incomes
   c. Rates of absolute poverty
   d. Shrinking social expenditure by the Government

ii. Process indicators
   a. The amount of services offered
   b. Introduction of fee for previously free services e.g., health and education
   c. Cut in subsidies on basic items such as food
   d. A qualitative rather than quantitative decline in services

iii. Outcome indicators
   a. Infant mortality rate
   b. Deterioration in nutrition indicators
   c. Stagnant or deteriorating health conditions

iv. Behavioral indicators
   a. Child labor
   b. Child abandonment and vagrancy
   c. Youth delinquency
   d. Female-headed households.

A Few General Relations:

1. Linkages:
   a. Decline in employment, wages, or both, leading to reduced incomes
   b. Inflation, particularly for food
   c. Cuts in social expenditure
   d. Overall deterioration of income distribution

2. Multipliers
   a. "Even a relatively modest drop in GNP or other economic changes in the industrialized countries can have forbidding consequences for large groups of poor people and their children in trade - and financially dependent developing countries. This amplification of negative effects is a result of several multipliers." (Jolly and Cornea: 218)

3. Time Lags
   a. "There are time lags between the inception of the economic recession and the point at which deterioration in child welfare and survival become apparent." (Ibid: 219).

I present some general data, which basically shows that every element in the model has been affected by the impact of globalization on children's welfare.

The State of the Children and their Families

According to a World Bank study, 1.4 billion people lived in extreme poverty in 2005. Twenty-seven per cent of children under five in the developing world were underweight. Their mortality rate was 83 per 1,000 live births, about 14 times the rate in rich nations. (New York Times, Sept 9, 2008). In some countries of the sub-Saharan Africa, 17 per cent of newborns do not live to the age of 5 (Sengupta, 2002).

The UNICEF document, State of the World's Children 2008, reminds us that the number of deaths per 1000 live births in developing countries varies from 27 (in Latin America and the Caribbean) to 160 in the sub-Saharan region.

It is pointed out that about 60 million children in India under the age of six live below the poverty line and every second child in the country is malnourished. Almost two million children in India die every year before reaching their first birthday. One in 11 dies before their fifth birthday. Hundreds of thousands of children die every year from preventable diseases like diarrhoea. Children of 100 million families live without water at home. The woes go on.

According to the Inter-American Institute of the Child, 15 million of the region's roughly 200 million children live on the streets and six million are malnourished. Moreover, 70 per cent of the victims of violence are minors, mainly girls (Rodriguez, 1998).

Economic dimensions of globalization and impact on children

It is obvious that one of the primary benefits of globalization, with its liberalization policies and promotion of international trade, is the rise in living standards for the many or few. In some countries, rising gross domestic product (GDP) has brought better health care and education for children. But while poverty rates have decreased in some countries, worldwide, the actual number of people living in poverty increased by 100 million in the 1990s (Stigliz, 2002a: 5) . Further, there is growing income inequality.

In a study on globalization, childhood poverty and education in the Americas by Mickelson and others (2000), they noted that globalization and the intertwined political economies of Latin American countries and the United States simultaneously create wealth and poverty in all three nations. While the causes and conditions of poverty differ, street and homeless children in Brazil, Cuba and the United States invariably stand as extreme manifestations of that poverty. On the basis of case studies and micro analyses, they came to the conclusion that neoliberal structural adjustments contribute to increased income polarizations within and among nations. They exacerbate the extant structures of inequality, increasing the pressures that lead children to work and live on the streets.

And as concluding remarks they point out: "The presence of homeless and street children within sight of the skyscrapers, museums, and luxury apartments of great North and South American cities exposes the contradictions between the concentration of wealth and the intensification of poverty that accompany globalization." (Ibid: 280)

In a similar vein, looking at Mexico and Thailand, Chujar (2004: 1), remarked "Experiences from across the world show that children are among the most at risk when local economies are opened up to global market forces without making adequate investments and safeguards, especially for the poor and marginalized. World Bank reports analysing the effects in Mexico and Thailand of the financial crisis due to exposure to global markets, found that children were withdrawn from school, entered hazardous jobs and prostitution rings, and suffered from development damage due to malnutrition."

Indian experience

According to Chaujar (2004) policies of liberalization and privatization in India are supposed to have affected children at two levels.

1. At the level of the impact of the reforms on livelihood and food security of the poor, especially rural agrarian communities: Heightened livelihood insecurity and cuts in food subsidies have forced many children out of school and into work to augment family income.
2. At the level of the impact of reforms on Government spending on social sectors such as health and education: Commercialization of health and education and decreased State investment in improving access and quality of these services have further deprived large numbers of marginalized children of the opportunity to improve their education and health status.

Latin American experience

A UNICEF-sponsored seminar (1998) concluded that economic globalization has failed to reduce, and in some cases has even exacerbated, the social ills plaguing children in Latin America. The economic model predominant in the region and the process of globalization accompanying it today accentuate the poor distribution of income, poverty and unequal access to social services and food security. According to the Inter-American Institute of the Child, 15 million of the region's roughly 200 million children live on the streets and six million are malnourished. Moreover, 70 per cent of the victims of violence are minors, mainly girls. According to the ILO, some 17.5 million children in the region work, a large proportion of them in domestic service, especially in Brazil and Venezuela.

Child labor

Globalization reduces child labor in Vietnam, declared one report (NBER working Paper No. 8760 quoted in Davis, 2008). Contrary to the popular belief that a globalized marketplace will increase child labor in Vietnam, households appear to have taken advantage of higher income after the rice price increase to reduce child labor despite increased earning opportunities for children (Davis, 2008). A similar experience was reported by Neymayer et al. (2005) and Eric and Soys (2008) saying that globalization is associated with less, not more, child labor.

An ILO study (quoted in Workshop. No.2. Globalization, Liberalization and child labor, 1997) points to the use of child labor in the carpet industry in India. Adverse public opinion in industrialized countries resulted in pressure on importers and Governments to penalize countries that allow child labor. The private sector has taken a number of measures in terms of preparing codes of conduct in concrete instances like football manufacturing in Pakistan using children. In recent years, voluntary codes of conduct have increasingly been adopted by importing firms and multinational corporations based in the United States. This can be attributed to the awareness in these firms of their social responsibilities and to their understandable desire to project a favorable image and to maintain, if not increase, their market share.

Deterioration in child welfare was documented in eight countries in Latin America, 16 in sub-Saharan Africa, three in North Africa and the Middle East, and four in South and East Asia (Vasanthi Raman, 200http://www.oecd.org/dataoecd/0/44/39530659.pdf8, 1997).

> "The most obvious contribution globalization is making to the increase in child labour is its intensification of price competition for global consumer markets…to have child labour means lower costs, because the wages are very low, children never complain, and they work long hours with no overtime pay" (Weissman,1997).

Effect of globalization on children's mental health

A study by Sami Timimi (2005) pointed out that globalization is resulting in inappropriate domination of the Western view of mental health as well as of economic approaches. And this promotes individualism, weakens social ties, and creates ambivalence toward children. Values such as duty, responsibility, and a community orientation found in many non-Western cultures may promote psychiatric well-being. Exporting Western child rearing beliefs and psychiatric practices to developing countries is undermining local values, beliefs and practices. In fact, the study suggests that non-Western cultures can provide new ideas to enrich child psychiatric theory and practice.

Cultural homogenization

One of the most powerful impacts of globalization is the cultural homogenization that is taking place along with economic globalization. With this, there is an increasing ability to influence the lives of the people all over the world intentionally or recklessly.

> *"Globalization represents a very real challenge for cultural diversity because of the risks of Standardization and impoverishment inherent in the increasing commercialisation of cultural goods and services which impinges on creativity and cultural innovation."* (Extract 04014 from UNESCO's Draft Program 20042005, see UNESCO, 2003).

In fact, in terms of impact, the cultural dimension is far more detrimental to humanity than the economic process itself. The Information Communication Technology (ICT), and the media and entertainment industry in particular, help this process. MTV is probably one of the most dramatic symbols of this.

Cultural homogenization is the belief that the so-called global culture follows the global economy and this has led to such phrases as "Cocacolonization" and "McDonaldization." The notion of "McDonaldization" refers to the "worldwide homogenization of societies through the impact of multinational corporations." In this view, the mechanisms for change are closely linked with the globalization of the market economy and multinational corporations. As Holton (2000: 142) notes, "consumer capitalism of this type has been built upon a standardized brand image, mass advertising, and the high status given by many Third World populations to Western products and services." This view of cultural homogenization and the global economy has been strengthened by the rise of the Internet and other information technologies. With the influence of Information Communication Technology, computers, and the Internet, the world becomes a small and new place that directs children, especially immigrant children, toward exploring actions, events and virtual groups. According to Giddens (1991, p. 187), children have "phenomenal worlds that are for the most part truly global." Robertson (1992, p.8) argued that children today gradually develop "the intensification of consciousness of the world as a whole." Tomlinson (1999, p. 30) wrote that the world as a whole "increasingly exists as a cultural horizon within which we (to varying degrees) frame our existence." This means in developing a global identity, children have a sense of belonging to a worldwide culture which includes an awareness of the events, practices, styles, and information that are part of the global culture. The global identity of children allows them to use information technology to communicate with people throughout the world. Tomlinson (1991) believes that children are not passive recipients (quoted from the literature review by Loshini Naidoo).

The World of Internet, video games, mobile phones, IPods…

The data is primarily from the Western world. But the upper classes of the developing world have very similar experiences. What should interest us is the question: what happens to culturally homogenized children who sing the same songs, hear the same stories, eat the same food, and dream the same dreams? Not all that the children are watching is social, educational, or fun in its original sense. It would not be an exaggeration to say that through this intense exposure to the Internet, video games and other media, children are well formed to be citizens of a consumerist society, devoid of social sensibilities and concern for the other or the universe.

Research findings vary and are not always conclusive. But there is enough evidence to show that video games stimulate aggressive behaviors, affect social behavior and show negative influence on logical thinking, besides influencing school behavior.

Toward a response

Globalization has not given children much hope. In spite of limited experiences of benefits and successes, the larger scenario is one of discrimination, marginalization, and denial of basic rights to children.

Structural changes are critical for bringing about a change in the situation. Reaching information to people (Indian context: Right to Information), awareness creation, and organizing for collective action are important in bringing about structural changes through influencing governance and policies. The state must be held responsible for providing the basic rights of children. At the macro level, strong alliances are required to influence and impact national and international policies. The role of international bodies such as the UN, UNICEF, ILO, and various international NGOs is critical too.

The UN Millennium Development Goals for children had set out concrete improvements in such areas as infant and maternal mortality, child poverty, and child labor. While the steps to these goals were clear, it has not been easy to implement these. In fact, data shows that aid from developed countries fell by almost 13 per cent between 2005 and 2007, jeopardizing the performance of Millennium Development Goals. (New York Times, Sept 9, 2008). The UNICEF assessment says that East Asia and Pacific, Latin America and the Caribbean, CEE/CIS, and the industrialized territories are on track, while the sub-Saharan area, the Middle East and North Africa, South Asia, and the developing countries on the whole are lagging in their efforts to achieve this goal.

Perhaps the most important response is "not to lose sight of children themselves…to listen to them…because they will be the best informants about what it is like to grow up in the Mississippi Delta, the slums of Mumbai, or the *favelas* of Sao Paulo. These children's life stories will remind us why we have an intellectual and a moral responsibility to summon all our energies to analyze those forces and conditions which leave so many children behind" (Rizzini and Bush, 2002; Fass, 2003).

References

Chaujar, Paro. (2004). 'Globalization – will our children pay the price?' Paper presented at the World Social Forum. Mumbai.

Fass, Paula. (2007). 'Children of a New World: Society, Culture and Globalization. New York: New York University Press.

Jolly R. and Cornia A. G. (Eds). (1984). 'The impact of world recession on Children'. Oxford: Pergamon Press.

Loshini Naidoo: Rupture or continuity? *Transnational Curriculum Inquiry* 4 (1) 2007 http://nitinat.library.ubc.ca/ojs/index.php/tci20)

Mickelson, Roslyn, A. (Ed). (2000). 'Children on the Streets of the

Americas: Globalization, Homelessness and Education in the United States, Brazil and Cuba. London: Routledge.
Rizzini and Bush. (2002). 'Editorial: Globalization and children' in Childhood. London: Sage Publications. Vol. 9(4): pp. 371–374
Weissman, Robert. (1997). 'Stolen Youth: Brutalized children, Globalization and the Campaign to end Child Labour' in Multinational Monitor, January/February. pp 10–16.

CHAPTER EIGHT

THE IMPACT OF PARENTS' MIGRATION ON CHILDREN

CAROLINE S. DE LEON

Introduction

The objective of this article is to present the impact of absent overseas parents on the children they left behind, based on data in the Philippine context.

In Asia, the Philippines is the major supplier of labor migrants to over 100 countries. More than eight million, or 10% of the 85 million Filipinos are working overseas as nurses, caregivers, teachers, construction workers, engineers, seafarers, and domestic workers (Reyes, 2007). Seventy-two per cent of the migrants are women who are employed mainly in the Middle East and other parts of Asia, such as Hong Kong and Singapore (Parrenas, 2010).

Commonly known as Overseas Filipino Workers (OFWs), these migrants go overseas to fulfil some specific task and then return to their countries of origin upon expiration of their contracts. Travel home to visit the family is difficult and can be undertaken only depending on savings and permission from employers. Nevertheless, some migrant workers are able to go home every two years.

The primary reason for working abroad is to escape poverty and earn a better income so that their children can have a good education. It is estimated that there are approximately nine million children under the age of 18 who are left behind by one or both parents who go overseas to work (Reyes, 2007).

On average, mothers leave to work overseas when their children are between five and nine years old, while with overseas fathers, children are slightly younger.

The Social Costs of Migration

Economic and physical

According to the Washington-based Population Reference Bureau (2008), remittances from OFWs make up about 10% of the country's gross domestic product. OFWs send home remittances of up to eight billion U.S. dollars a year.

A number of studies have shown that migration has brought about improved economic circumstances for the family in terms of adequate food, clothing, and better education. Findings, however, on whether remittances have any significant impact on the family's financial welfare, are inconsistent.

One study indicated that the remittances have not benefited low-income families as much as higher income families (Opiniano, 2008). The money sent back home was often insufficient to meet the needs of these families (Arellano et al, as cited in Reyes, 2007). Another finding was that children of OFWs are not necessarily better off in terms of health, as visits to doctors take place only when children have a medical emergency (Edillon, 2008). Social scientists have pointed out that while remittances may help with basic needs, the social and psychological costs far outweigh the financial benefits.

Family relationships

Family separation has a detrimental effect on both the quality of marital relationships, as well as the relationship between parents and children (Battistela & Conaco, 1996). Researchers believe that separation of the family due to migration can weaken the bonds of marital and family relationships.

How migration impacts the family left behind will vary depending on which parent migrates. When the father migrates, the mother, who traditionally has limited roles outside the home, is forced to assume increased responsibilities inside and outside the household. When the mother migrates, the husband is faced with the need to provide nurturing.

Most fathers may not be prepared for this role reversal and so will pass on the caregiving role to the eldest daughter or to the grandmother or other members of the household (Scalabrini Migration Center, 2003). However, some fathers were found to be more open to role reversal and engaged in more cooking, cleaning, and childcare work than would normally be the case for a Filipino male.

In general, the absence of parents owing to migration upsets the equilibrium in the family system, as it creates drastic changes in family structure and family roles, especially when both parents work abroad. Such disruptions are felt more when it is the mother rather than the father who works abroad.

Given a choice, children prefer their father to work abroad rather than their mother (Anonuevo & Guerra, as cited in Bryant, 2005). They feel that their mothers are more competent to perform the duties of both mother and father to the family.

It is ironic that mothers leave their children behind to care for other women's children. Upon her return, she may feel heartbroken when she realizes that she has become a stranger in her own home.

Whether it is the father or mother who migrates, some children even blame their absent parent as a contributory factor to their behavioral problems such as drug use and poor performance in school (Bryant, 2005).

Psychological and social

The continuing exodus of mothers to take up jobs overseas affects the psychological and social development of children they leave behind. A number of studies suggest that children face greater psychological damage and risk when it is the mother who decides to work overseas (Parrenas, 2006).

Children of migrant mothers, even if they are showered with material benefits, still consider the migration of their mother as a form of abandonment (Parrenas, 2010).

Although they may be directly told that their mother's leaving is to improve the family's financial situation, the children do not consider their mother's migration as a form of parental love and care. This is especially true in the case of prolonged maternal separation.

Mothers come home and stay for only two months at the most, then go back abroad if the contract is renewed. This separation–reunion cycle exacts an emotional toll from the children as they are aware of the temporary nature of the mother's presence, and once more experience feelings of abandonment, resentment, and anger.

Adolescents experience different emotional issues related to an absent migrant parent (Carandang, 2007). Sons who grow up without the presence and guidance of a father may develop gender identity problems, particularly during adolescence.

Those with absent mothers were found to harbor feelings of anger, confusion, anxiety, and loneliness (Battistela & Conaco, 1996). The feeling of neglect and abandonment is most felt by the eldest daughter, who assumes the mother's role in the family, particularly if the father is unable to take on the caregiving function. This added burden on the children can in turn affect school performance and social relationships.

Overseas parents are sometimes seen only as a source of gifts and money (Bryant, 2005). Their efforts in trying to compensate for their absence through material goods can develop in children a consumerist attitude and give them a distorted view of the value of migration. Some children see their migrant parent as a role model because they also have dreams of going abroad in the future (Anonuevo, 2002).

Children of migrants are also vulnerable to abuse and violence (Reyes, 2007) when the mother is absent, as seen from a case of a two-year-old child who was physically abused by his caregiver, a teenage uncle, who was a drug addict.

What Can Soften the Damaging Impact?

A few studies have shown that children are able to reasonably cope with their situation as long as there are "protective factors" to buffer the negative impact of parental absence. Aside from the social and emotional support from caregivers and extended family members, another key factor that can mitigate the impacts of transnational migration on children is regular and quality communication between overseas parents and their left behind children.

Given the reality of parent's migration and its negative repercussions on the well-being of children left behind, serious attention must be given to explore ways of sustaining and strengthening family relationships across distances.

One essential ingredient in nurturing the parental bond is regular quality communication wherein children are encouraged to voice out their thoughts and feelings regarding the situation they are in. and their day to day life. Steps must be taken to ensure that left-behind children do not remain invisible and voiceless victims but can be empowered to be resilient individuals with a sense of agency.

In the context of family separation due to parents 'migration children's rights as defined in the *United Nations Conventions on the Rights of the Child* should be recognised. As delineated in Articles 12 and 13, children have the right to express opinions and the right to freedom of expression and information on matters that affect them. When children's voices are heard and their views and feelings respected, they feel valued, worthwhile, are able to adapt better to difficult circumstances.

Studies have shown that overseas parents do maintain contact with their children through letters, phone calls, text-messages, and emails Regular communication lessens feelings of loneliness and anxiety of both migrant parents and children.

Advanced technology has also made it possible for more instantaneous and intimate contact, particularly through skype. Communication, however, has been found to be more instrumental than affective in nature focussing more on how remittances are spent, school progress, health, and discipline (Anonuevo, 2009), than the sharing of feelings and communication of affection.

There is need to promote sensitive communication which responds to the emotional needs of children left behind. Children need to hear directly from their parents that they are loved and appreciated .Children feel they are important when parents listen to what they have to say and show keen interest in their activities. Through quality parent-child communication, children can learn to view the separation as a means of discovering their inner resources of independence, resourcefulness, responsibility, and decision-making skills.

Key factors that can mitigate the impacts of transnational migration on children include the following:

- Clearly communicating to the children the reason for a parent's migration. However, acceptance of the parent's departure will depend on the maturity level and cognitive development of the child.
- Regular communication with children or caregivers through letters, phone calls, and e-mails lessens the feelings of loneliness and anxiety of both migrant parent and children.
- Social and emotional support from caregivers and extended family members can moderate the damaging effects of an absent parent.

Conclusion

Since migration is a social reality and will persist in the years to come, there must be special interventions to mitigate the risks children face. Findings from different studies clearly point to the importance of educating parents, guardians, and stakeholders on the multifaceted impact of migration on the well-being of children. One mode of intervention is in the form of pre-departure seminars and caregiving workshops, to increase awareness that children left behind have psychosocial needs that must be met and that their basic rights must be protected.

Counselling and support group programs for children of migrant parents, where they can share their feelings and experiences, can help strengthen children's self-esteem and interpersonal relationships, which are essential ingredients in their social adjustment.

The well-being of children left behind should be a continuing concern, and demands concerted efforts of government, NGOs, schools, church groups, and families.

References

An, E.D.(2009), *Addressing the social cost of migration in the Philippines: The Atikha experience*. Atikha Inc. http://www.icgmd.info/sessions/session_1_2/pdf..

Anonuevo, E. D. and Anonuevo, A. eds. (200) *Coming home: women, migration and reintegration.* Balikbayani Foundation, Inc and Atikha Overseas Workers and Communities Initiatives, Inc.

Battistela, G, and Conaco, C. (1996). Impact of migration on the children left behind. *Asian Migrant,* Vol. 9 Issue No. 3.

Bryant, J. (2005). *Children of international migrants in Indonesia, Thailand, and the Philippines: a review of evidence and policies.* Inocenti Working Paper, UNICEF.

Edillon, R.G. (2008). *The effects of parent's migration on the rights of Children left behind..* Asia Pacific Policy Center, UNICEF.

Opiniano, J. (2008). Stories of faraway Filipinos. *OFW Journalism Consortium.*

Parreflas, Rhacel Salazar (2006) *Children of Global Migration: Transnational Families and Gendered Woes.* Manila, Ateneo de Manila University Press

Parrenas, R.S. (2005). Long distance intimacy: Class, gender and intergenerational relations between mothers and children in Filipino transnational families. Global Networks.5(4), pp 317-36..

Population Reference Bureau. (2008). World Population Data Sheet. www.prb.org/pdf08/08WPDS_Eng.pdf. Behind, Working Paper, United Nations Children's Fund (August).

Reyes, M. (2008). Migration and Filipino children left behind: A literature review. *United Nations Children's Fund,* Scalabrini Migration Center, Overseas Workers Welfare Administration (2004). *Hearts apart; migration in the eyes of the Filipino children.* Episcopal Commission for the Pastoral Care of Migrants and Intinerant People -CBCP/Apostolship of the Sea –Manila: Quezon City.

CHAPTER NINE

IMPACT OF VIOLENCE ON CHILDREN

WERNER TSCHAN

The universal need of children

"*Give me back my childhood*!" was a cry from an adult person during a survivor workshop, when this person realized that it was not normal to be neglected. This example does not come from India, but from a Western nation. Violence and neglect happen worldwide and constitute a global burden. It is difficult for survivors to talk about what they did not experience, because often they are not aware of the other reality which is guaranteed by the Convention of the Rights of the Child (CRC) and which is thankfully the norm for many of us. Growing up in a violence-free environment is a human right—it is a salient precondition for healthy development.

We may ask ourselves whether there really are distinct physical, mental, verbal, and emotional aspects of abuse in the family context—or whether they go hand in hand. Does a child who is sexually abused by his father, by his mother, by his siblings, by members of the extended family, only suffer from the sexualized violence per se? Is sexual abuse by a family member possible without emotional abuse? We have to rethink our approaches to this topic and the language we use to describe what happens.

All forms of violence within the family context lead to poly-victimization (Finkelhor 2008). The most salient traumatic factor is the loss of a secure attachment relationship, for example, the loss of the father figure or mother figure—even in cases when the attachment figure is incapable of protecting the child from being abused. These children are "children without childhood," those who do not have a parent to play with, who do not have a parent who provides them with a positive role model, and who do not have a parent who takes care of them.

Children without childhood are a sad reality both in the East and the West—all over the world (Ferguson et al. 1999). It is a global problem. The needs of children are universal—whether you are born as an Inuit, as a Hindu, as a Maori, as a child from a European background, or as a child growing up in a township. The primary need is universal: the need for a secure base to enable a healthy development (Bowbly 1988) next to other basic needs such as nutrition, shelter, clothes, education, and so on. Children suffer from devastating developmental problems when they do not have the safe environment they need (Glaser 2000). Affective neuroscience clearly documents the outcome when a child does not have a secure base (Panksepp 1998).

Preparing for parenthood

Children are threatened from the beginning by the condition of their parents—what affects the parents affects the offspring (Finkelhor 1984). Human beings are dependent on their caregivers not just in physical terms but also in emotional terms.

I focus on facts provided by Attachment Theory (Bowlby 1988) and Psychotraumatology to understand the needs of offspring and the traumatic results, when these conditions are not provided.

Decades ago, medical professionals rejected the fathers' presence at childbirth for a variety of reasons. The number of men present through their partners' labor has increased to nearly 100% today in Western countries. What has become evident is that women who have their partners present during birthing suffer less pain, need less medication, and have shorter labors (Niven 1985). Fathers attending the birth of their baby feel confirmed in fatherhood and often reported that the experience facilitated a close relationship with the child, and that their involvement in the day-to-day care of their baby was easier (Palkovitz 1987). To be involved in the birth process and antenatal care often gives fathers the feeling of being the parent and not just the provider, which helps to reinforce both the role of fathers and male role-taking. Finally, fathers must realize that they are involved in the pregnancy not only for the benefit of their partner and the baby but also for themselves.

The birth of a baby initiates a time of transition and it is just the beginning of major change in the life of the child's parents. There is no question that the mother is the one most profoundly affected. We fully agree with Ball (1995), when he states: "as childbirth is such a common experience, it is perhaps easy to overlook the tremendous and unique changes which it brings." Contrary to the general joy and delight related to the offspring, the process of pregnancy and parenthood leads to a series of losses: loss of control over one's physical state, loss of control over lifestyle and the loss of sleep which caring for a small baby brings (Ball 1995). The tremendous changes require a period of adjustment and adaptation. The birth of a baby is not only the beginning of the infant's life, but it is also a major life-change for the entire family and the wider society. In most cultures, the birth is marked by a variety of rituals and rites of passage. This is mirrored in the Congress' subtitle: "*The transforming role of the family in a global society.*"

Postnatal care and outcome studies usually focus on the mother and her baby. When the father is considered, in most cases it is as an absentee. In Western counties the number of single-parent families or functional single-parent families (due to the absence of one parent, in most cases the father) has increased over the years and is estimated to touch the 50% rate soon. Fathers-to-be, especially first-time-fathers, often suffer from Couvades syndrome. The prevalence varies from 10% to over 60% (Khanobdee et al. 1993). Men suffer from postnatal depression up to 9% (Ballard et al. 1994). Several risk factors identified for women as increasing the likelihood of postnatal depression, are directly related to their partners' mental health, for example, poor marital relationship and lack of social support. Again, there is an abundance of literature examining postnatal depression in women, but not in their male partners. Studies suggest that non-depressed partners may buffer the effects on infants having depressed mothers (Hossain et al. 1994). The quality of the relationship is an important source for the woman's well-being, and caregivers should therefore encourage both parents to discuss any difficulties they may be having in the transition to parenthood.

Although positive aspects will counterbalance the stress provoked by any major life change, some fail in the transition process. The satisfaction of personal needs produces a state of emotional security, which can be described as an internal feeling—a state of confidence and emotional well-being. When the normal mechanisms for dealing with changes are not effective, some degree of stress will be experienced. Postnatal depression (onset within one year of childbirth) is the most common mental health problem after childbearing, affecting approximately 10–15% of all women. The baby blues have a considerable impact both on the new-born (Grace et al. 2003), as on the mother and the family. Young infants are highly sensitive to the quality of care they receive, and the child's brain development depends directly on the interaction with the family (Glaser 2000). Data on psychosocial interventions clearly indicate that prevention of postnatal depression by offering intervention courses such as "preparing for parenthood" is effective (Wheatley et al. 2003).

Balancing needs
- Individual internal needs (desire for approval and achievement)
- External demands and expectations of behavior (peer values, culture, society)

The coping process as described by Lazarus (1969).

The coping process illustrates how a person responds to change. Lazarus places great emphasis on the need to understand the coping process in the context of the individual's environment and the sociocultural support someone receives.

To remain realistic, it is important to consider data from young urban adolescent girls who often suffer from a compounded community trauma, with a high proportion of them become teenage mothers. In interviewing these young mothers, Horowitz et al. (1995) reported that: "Only in their relationship with their young baby they are able to experience a zone of safety, connectedness, and trust otherwise missing in their lives." Just referring them to a psychiatrist does not work. "The high rate of avoidance symptoms noted in these adolescent girls is one indicator of the unlikelihood that they would seek or accept standard psychiatric treatment ..." (Horowitz et al. 1995).

Sex offenses are generally thought of as being committed by men. There is increasing knowledge about female sexual offenders (Cavanagh Johnson 1989). At the same time, in her article Cavanagh Johnson noted that 100% of the examined females who molested children had been previously sexually violated, 85% of them by family members. Despite the fact that articles from 50 years ago had already pointed out that incest is far more prevalent in our society that one would estimate (Raphling et al. 1967), the vast majority of professionals tended to ignore disturbing facts. To simply expect that women will disclose things such as maternal–neonatal incest is unrealistic. However, such things do happen, as unbelievable as it may sound.

As professionals involved in developmental issues, our understanding should be founded on facts rather than on general assumptions. We should take note of these facts, which help us to enlarge our understanding of certain problems. Most of the knowledge about the associations of sexual trauma and the impact on personal development has been gained through therapeutically working with both victims and offenders. The professional community should take note of these findings, because there is increasing evidence that a history of sexual violence constitutes a major risk factor for the development of severe mental problems (Heim et al. 2001, 2002).

A mother once told me during a treatment session: "*The abuser of my son not only abused my loved one but he also abused the whole family*." Sexualized violence always has an impact on associated victims as well. Partners of victims of sexualized violence need help and support, often to a greater extent than the effort for the direct victim. The lack of general awareness of their situation and the help offered to these associated victims is often minimal.

The family as a place of violence: prenatal, natal, and postnatal traumas

The vast majority of interpersonal violence takes place within the (extended) family environment. There are four main avenues that lead to psychological problems related to pregnancy and delivery: (1) sexual violence, (2) physical violence, (3) emotional violence, and (4) abuse and neglect. The detection of traumatic events in patient histories is in most cases difficult for a variety of reasons. The majority of patients usually do not consider a link between their actual symptoms and the past traumatic experiences, which often happened years, if not decades, ago. Furthermore, feelings of shame, loyalty, and guilt often undermine the ability to openly disclose what had happened to women, further increased by the fear of not being believed or being blamed. The diagnostic procedure always rests with the clinician; therefore, the creation of a trustworthy doctor–patient relationship is the main precondition for disclosing these experiences. The duty to build up and maintain a "secure base" is one of the physician's first tasks. The posttraumatic stress disorder (PTSD) concept can serve as a model to diagnose these effects: Is there a relation between the current symptoms and past traumatic and threatening experiences, which leads to a functional impairment? This approach is illustrated by the following figure:

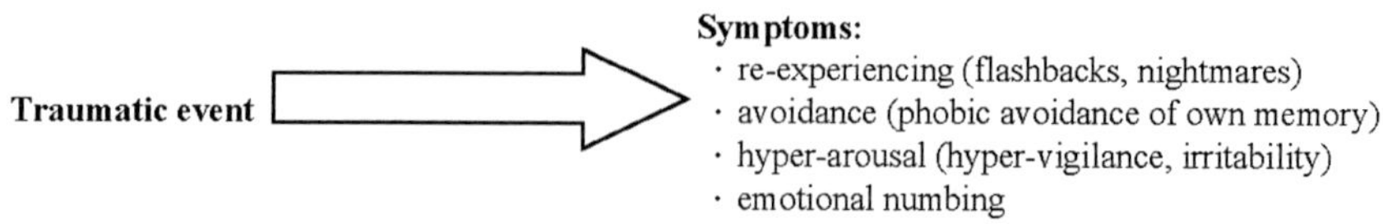

Aside from the exposure to one or more traumatic events, the diagnosis requires a characteristic response, such as intense fear, helplessness, or horror, and the symptoms must lead to a significant distress or functional impairment. There was reluctance among health professionals to acknowledge that PTSD can also occur following childbirth when women have not been offered appropriate treatment (Lyons 1998). Kitzinger (1992, quoted in Lyons) proposed that there are similarities between traumatic obstetric experiences and the experience of sexual assault. In childbirth, as in rape, a woman may be stripped, forcibly exposed, her legs splayed and tethered, and her sexual organs put on display to all comers. The woman is no longer in control of her own body and of her intimacy. This may trigger horrifying past experiences such as sexual abuse histories.

However, in most cases of severe and repeated trauma during childhood, the psychological response is different from this simplified pathogenic model as suggested by the PTSD concept. This is mainly related to the fact that family members who commit a sexual crime against their offspring are simultaneously in the position of care-givers. The results are complex and chronic traumatic experiences. Therefore the outcome is characterized by polytraumatization, which can be diagnosed as dissociative identity disorder (DID), personality disorder, depression, psychosis, substance abuse, somatic problems such as eating disorders, chronic pain disorder, fibromyalgia, chronic urogenital problems, and so on. The link to severe trauma in all these diagnostic entities is based on rather new results—mainly stimulated by research following the implementation of PTSD and DID since 1980.

How common traumatic experiences such as sexualized violence are depends on how violence is defined. If someone uses a narrowly defined approach or includes noncontact experiences such as exhibitionistic behavior, this leads to a great variation in research findings. The recently published World Report on Violence and Health by the WHO (Krug et al. 2002) estimates that about 20% of all women worldwide, and up to 10% of all men, suffer sexual violence as children or adolescents. Russel (1983,

1986) reported in a study that 38% women in the sample had suffered sexualized violence involving physical contact, whereas the figure was 54% when experiences involving noncontact abuse were included. Therefore, we agree with Rodgers et al. (2003): "Given the high prevalence of sexual trauma, it is likely that a substantial proportion of pregnant women have been victims of sexual trauma at some point in their lives."

Several authors have studied the impact of domestic and sexual violence during pregnancy itself. According to epidemiological findings, pregnancy is a high-risk period during which violence may begin or escalate. Rates up to 20% of all pregnant women experiencing violent acts have been reported. Violence during pregnancy is associated with adverse maternal conditions, which may also have a direct or indirect influence on the foetus. Such influence is documented with:

- self-induced or attempted abortions
- spontaneous miscarriages
- divorce and separation during pregnancy
- secondary psychological problems like alcohol and drug abuse
- maternal antenatal hospitalization
- labor and delivery complications
- higher rates of caesarean delivery
- preterm birth
- low birth weight
- postnatal complications.

In the aftermath of pregnancy and birth, some other problems arise. Holding the newborn baby in her arms, a woman with a history of sexualized violence can suddenly gain a shocking awareness of her own vulnerability, when she was sexually violated as a child, either by a male or a female. Even more hidden and disturbing are instances of sexualized violence by females.

The magnitude of abuse in the family context

A generation ago we learned that incest is an absolutely rare phenomenon. Prominent experts in the field estimated the magnitude of sexual violence within the family context as being around one in a million children – it was seen as a tragic exception. It was the feminist movement which raised the curtain: today we know better. The family context is the place where most violence happens, and both adults and children are at a much greater risk of experiencing violence and neglect in the family than elsewhere. But still, today much is hidden behind a wall of silence, and family is considered a private matter—scientific research is contributing to this silence by not asking the right questions. When epidemiological studies about sexual abuse are carried out, in most cases men are not questioned about their experiences—by simply not asking the relevant questions, we never have the figures to analyze the situation, which then biases our view of the reality. The lack of figures is taken to mean that the problem does not exist—there is no problem of male victimization. The same is true for domestic violence (Dutton 2006), where most studies focus on female victims and male offenders, and therefore overlook the opposite fact, that males suffer the same amount of traumatization and that the number of female offenders is comparable to the male situation. By simply not asking the right questions you may still believe that planet Earth is the center of the universe, and that the sun and the stars are rotating around it. When it comes to violence, the family can no longer be considered a private matter, because violence affects the entire society.

Rape in marriage was not regarded as a crime until the end of the 20th century, when finally, under pressure from the feminist movement, the law was changed in a more or less simultaneous worldwide process. Only by implementing this law did women have a chance to protect their rights of emotional and bodily integrity. A similar development can be seen with the implementation of anti-harassment laws within the last three decades. Sexual abuse at the workplace was long considered a man's affair. The shift of awareness goes hand in hand with the implementation process of specific laws and, on the other hand, only this implementation provides the clear understanding that certain behavior is a crime. Smacking children is a violation of their bodily integrity, and therefore not acceptable. Only a few countries have banned corporal punishment of children—the good news is that the number of nations creating adequate laws is growing and this contributes to stopping the transgenerational circle of violence. In reality, physical punishment has often served as an excuse for violent behavior—as long as society gives permission for this, it legitimates violence toward children. This lesson is learned early in life. Physical violence serves as a model for understanding the other forms of inacceptable behavior, such as emotional and mental abuse, including neglect, which is probably the most prevalent form of abuse.

As long as children were regarded as "belongings" of their parents, abuse could not be imagined—one cannot abuse something one owns. Children had no human rights. It took nearly a century to conceptualize the CRC (United Nations, 2007). Before 1989, the child was not regarded as a subject of its own rights. Despite the universal declaration of human rights during the time of the Enlightenment, children (and women) were not regarded as human beings. It was a long journey until the CRC was adopted by 191 nations, making it the most widely accepted treaty in the world! To give the weakest member of society a legal status and rights was an important precondition to realize the amount of traumatization children still suffer.

Article 19 of the Convention stipulates: "1. States Parties shall take all appropriate legislative, administrative, social and educational measures to protect the child from all forms of physical or mental violence, injury or abuse, neglect or negligent treatment, maltreatment or exploitation, including sexual abuse, while in the care of parent(s), legal guardian(s) or any other person who has the care of the child. 2. Such protective measures should, as appropriate, include effective procedures for the establishment of social programs to provide necessary support for the child and for those who have the care of the child, as well as for other forms of prevention and for identification, reporting, referral, investigation, treatment and follow-up of instances of child maltreatment described heretofore, and, as appropriate, for judicial involvement." The implications of Article 19 are numerous. In Article 27 the CRC claims that States Parties recognize the right of every child to a standard of living adequate for the child's physical, mental, spiritual, moral and social development.

In a nationwide survey, Ireland explored the magnitude of sexual violence—the data is published and known as the SAVI report (McGee et al: Sexual Abuse and Violence in Ireland, 2002). As much as 42% of women and 28% of men reported being sexually abused. A third of all women and a quarter of men experienced sexual abuse in their childhood (defined as less than 17 years of age). It is not the place here to discuss the available data on child sexual abuse, but these figures give an idea of the magnitude—every third girl and every fourth boy suffers from childhood sexual violence in a Western nation. Yet, today, silence covers this tragic reality, which not only affects the life of those abused but also of their families. Victims still hesitate to disclose what has been done to them. Society needs to listen.

Increasing awareness among the professional community

The understanding of the traumatic effects of abuse is another chapter in the development of mankind. Surprisingly, only in 1980 did medicine create simultaneously two new diagnostic categories for traumatic experiences—the PTSD and DID. It was the American Psychiatric Association who coined the two terms—after pressure from Vietnam Veterans and from rape victims (Herman 1992). Yet, even now, there are endless debates and controversies among professionals about the subject. Over thirty years after the implementation of these concepts it is still estimated that only a small percentage of those affected are diagnosed correctly. Obviously, society is still in denial about the effect of violence and neglect on children and its impact on health later. As long as there is no diagnosis, there is no acknowledgment of suffering; therefore, the impact on the health condition and economic burden is carried by those affected, thus creating another trauma and perpetuating the suffering. The following quotation illustrates the situation: "In psychiatry, each generation seems to have a need to formulate psychological phenomena in a new language—to find a contemporary voice, in keeping with the political tenor of the times. However, though this continual reinvention of the psychological wheel may make for interesting careers, it does not foster a solid accumulation of knowledge or the development of an effective treatment repertoire" (Van der Kolk et al. 1996, p. 67).

A landmark contribution was the book by Henry Kempe—"The Battered Child"—in 1968, when for the first time medicine recognized the impact of abuse on the development of the child. This paradigm shift is considered the turning point—when medicine began to acknowledge the existence of intrafamilial violence. Although many earlier contributions exist, they did not have such a landslide effect. A century before Kempe's publication, there was another landmark contribution by the French physician Ambroise Tardieu, who in 1857 edited the first medical book on sexualized violence and the link to incest committed within families and childcare institutions. Despite the fact that he later became one of the most influential physicians of his time, the resistance against facing reality was still overwhelming. Even today, despite the facts we have gleaned from over thirty years of research on trauma, psychiatric textbooks hardly cover violence and its impact on later development (see for example: http://www.ACEstudy.org). Against clear evidence, the extent of violence and its far reaching impact remain widely underestimated within the professional community.

The Secure Base

While growing up, human beings are dependent on other humans for survival. The care for the offspring is usually provided by family members. The attachment between the child and its caregiver can be regarded as a social umbilical cord, which is as essential for survival as other life conditions such as environmental conditions, clean water, nutrition, and housing. The legal and scientific distinctions between the different forms of abuse—physical, mental, verbal, emotional—are misleading, because the affected child always suffers from a combination of these effects. Sexualized violence may illustrate this, when, in cases of a complete absence from physical harm, the sexually violated child suffers from the loss of the persons to whom he/she is attached, from emotional disturbances, and the effects of these on brain development. We can see the same in cases of physical violence, which also affects the brain development of the child due to resulting stress reactions and their impact on neurobiological structures.

Attachment experiences during childhood contribute significantly to the development of self-esteem and identity (self); and the handling of relationships later in life (Fonagy 2002). There is a significantly increased risk of violent behavior in those who have experienced an unsecure attachment. Their infantile craving for secure attachment figures may lead to coercive and violent behavior (it is often their only coping mechanism to create social bonds); they have no inner moral limits because of the absence of positive role models; and the dynamic of the "identification with the aggressor" serves as a powerful mechanism in order to cope with their own violent experiences. Around a quarter of all sexually violated male children become offenders later in their lives. If we do not stop the inner- and intergenerational circle of violence, we contribute to the creation of future superpredators (Levy et al. 1998, 2000). It is essential for society to concentrate its energy on ensuring that the preconditions are met for creating a "secure base" for all children (Krug et al. 2002). The CRC sets down the framework on which we must build! Past experiences haunt those affected throughout their lives. (Van der Hart et al. 2006).

It's time for action!

Although it will never be possible to prevent every single individual from experiencing violence, it is important that our communities address the issue and provide all possible resources to avoid the traumatization of our children. The huge economic burden is carried by future generations.

Following is a list of helpful strategies:

- Care facilities for children (day school, leisure time activities)
- Child commissioners
- Social support networks
- Campaigns for educating parents
- School programs to educate children about their rights
- Education about sexuality and violence
- Adequate laws as a last resort remedy against violent parents
- Legal sanctions against smacking children
- Sex-offender register
- Therapeutic jurisprudence
- Treatment and training for violent offenders
- Child advocacy
- Treatment facilities for traumatized persons.

Children require freedom for healthy development. However, loss of clear boundaries, neglect, and a high amount of unstructured leisure time contribute significantly to criminal behavior in juveniles, according to a Swiss study. Societies must provide day schools and adequate leisure time structures for children.

Child commissioners (ombudsman) will help improve the situation of children. They reflect life conditions from the perspective of the child and may therefore contribute to improving childcare.

Social support networks contribute to improving the socioeconomic conditions of families in general. Intrafamilial tensions and stress are significantly reduced when the financial situation improves. Social support must be provided for the education and healthcare costs of children.

Parents have to be educated about the negative impact of abuse and neglect, and how to prevent these. Support facilities should be available to them.

Children have to learn about their rights, and possible sources for help and support. They also have the right to be educated about sexuality and violence—only then will they be able to recognize their right to say “NO”. Without reporting facilities, affected children will not be heard.

Adequate laws are considered a last resort against violent parents. Punishment is not supportive and should therefore only be used if all other possibilities have failed. The effect of such laws is more about raising awareness of the norms—for example, the banning of smacking children as a form of physical violence.

The sex-offender register and corresponding means are considered to be of great help in preventing traumatization of children. It helps in particular to avoid institutional violence—when children are taken into custody, whether it is within the school system, into "care," or within healthcare institutions. There is a balancing of rights between the assumption of innocence and the individual need for the security of children.

Traditionally, jurisprudence is not seen as a helping profession, because their first goal is to punish those who violate the law—a view focused on the past; whereas helping professions usually focus on future development. However, therapeutic jurisprudence emphasizes the psychological impact of law and jurisdiction, and is directed much more at future development then on past problems (Stolle et al. 2000). This is a fundamental paradigm shift which gives the law and jurisprudence a completely new basis for action (Gilligan 2001). Treatment and training programs for violent offenders must be in place.

Child advocates focus on the rights of children and ensure that governmental decisions are in accordance with children's needs.

The WHO has issued guidelines addressing medico-legal care for victims of sexual violence in 2003; emphasizing *that appropriate, good quality care should be available to all individuals who have been victims of sexual assault* (p.17). The report is critical about the fact that in at least *some cases, victims are subjected to multiple examinations in surroundings that do not meet minimum health standards* (WHO 2003, p.2). What is addressed here for sexualized violence is applicable for all forms of violence and neglect. Often, medical care is not focused on the particular needs of affected persons, and offers substandard care only.

Training of Professionals

One of the main preventive strategies is to educate and train professionals in the healthcare and educational sectors in order to make them fit for identifying (and for the healthcare sector: diagnosing and treating) affected children and parents. Traditional curricula do not cover the subject of innerfamilial violence, with the result that health care professionals are not prepared for diagnosing children affected by violence, nor are they prepared for adequate referral and treatment. By simply asking adequate questions, affected patients feel invited to talk about their past experiences. Many of them are silenced by their offenders. Survivors hesitate to talk about their experiences for a variety of reasons: they blame themselves; they may assume that nobody will believe a word they say. And last but not least, many of them do not see the relationship between their actual symptoms and their past traumatic experiences which may have happened a long time back in the past. It is the physicians' duty to clarify the issue and to provide adequate explanations for the actual situation.

I often compare this with the diagnosis of phantom pain. When, for example, a man who has lost his leg in an accident complains about cold toes, it is known as phantom pain. As long as physicians do not understand this phenomenon, they judge the patient to be deceptive and a liar. This is the effect of knowledge—derived from evidence-based results. It was the French researcher Pierre Janet who, in his doctoral dissertation in 1889, coined the term "psychological automatism" which describes the well-known fact that those affected by traumatic experiences show an increased reaction when confronted with the same situation. If you have experienced a violent situation as a child, similar conditions later in your life may trigger memories, and you react in the same way—because for you, the reality is still the same, when nobody believes you and nobody protects you. Survivors often have significant difficulty describing exactly what is going on; and many of them attempt to minimize their suffering.

Professional training and knowledge is a *sine qua non* condition for:

- Adequate questions
- Diagnostic approaches
- Helpful therapeutic intervention
- Initiating legal steps.

Professionals also have to know about secondary traumatization and the effect that facing atrocities has on their own health. Again, professional training is considered as a preventive strategy against the development of secondary traumatization.

Conclusion

Safeguarding all children from violence and neglect will never be possible (Gilligan 2001). However, society has various means to protect vulnerable children and to provide safer life conditions for all. The CRC obliges political decision makers to protect all children from atrocities. Children are innocent, and dependent on adult caretakers; all of them deserve safe conditions. The different intervention strategies in child abuse cases go hand in hand. Awareness of the magnitude of the different forms of violence and the long-lasting effects on children and families is the first step for decision makers to start intervention programs. The high prevalence of sexualized violence makes it likely that a substantial proportion of pregnant women have been victims of sexual trauma at some point in their lives. Increased physician monitoring of those women suffering from devastating life experiences may significantly reduce pregnancy complications and poor pregnancy outcomes. There is a clear need for curricular integration of sexual and interpersonal violence into medical formation and training.

The take-home message is: Prevention of the various forms of violence is possible. The resulting costs of preventive strategies must be balanced with the tremendous economic burden resulting from violence and neglect. If we help to stop violence in all forms, we contribute significantly to reducing the suffering of many children. It is time for action!

References

Ball JA: Reactions to motherhood. The role of postnatal care. Books for Midwives, Oxford.

Ballard CG, Davis R, Cullen PC, Mohan RN, Dean C. (1994). Prevalence of postnatal psychiatric morbidity in mothers and fathers. British Journal of Psychiatry, 164:782–788.

Bowlby J. (1988). A secure Base. London, Routledge,.

Cavanagh Johnson T. (1989). Female child perpetrators: children who molest other children. Child Abuse and Neglect; 13:571–585.

De Zulueta Felicity. (2006). From Pain to Violence. The traumatic roots of destructiveness. Chichester, John Wiley.

Dutton D. (2006). Rethinking domestic violence. Vancouver, University of British Columbia Press.

Fergusson David M., Mullen Paul E. (1999). Childhood Sexual Abuse. An Evidence Based Perspective. Thousand Oaks, Sage.

Finkelhor D. (1984). Child Sexual Abuse. New York, The Free Press.

Finkelhor David. (2008). Childhood Victimisation. Violence, crime, and abuse in the lives of young people. Oxford, Oxford University Press.

Fonagy P., György G., Jurist E.L., Target M. (2002). Affect regulation, Mentalization, and the Development of the Self. New York, Other Press.

Gilligan J. (2001). Preventing Violence. New York, Thames & Hudson.

Glaser D. (2000). Child abuse and neglect and the brain—A review. Journal of Child Psychology and Psychiatry, 41(1):97–118.

Grace SL, Evindar A, Stewart DE. (2003). The effect of postpartum depression on child cognitive development and behavior: A review and critical analysis of the literature. Arch Women's Mental Health; 6:263–274.

Heim C, Nemeroff CB. (2001). The role of childhood trauma in the neurobiology of mood and anxiety disorders: preclinical and clinical studies. Biol Psychiatry; 4 9:1023–1039.

Heim C, Newport DJ, Bonsall R, Miller AH, Nemeroff CB. (2001). Altered pituitary-adrenal axis responses to provocative challenge tests in adult survivors of childhood abuse. Am J Psychiatry, 158: 575–581.

Heim C, Newport DJ, Wagner D, Wilcox MM, Miller AH, Nemeroff CB. (2002). The role of early adverse experience and adulthood stress in the prediction of neuroendocrine stress reactivity in women: a multiple regression analysis. Depression and Anxiety, 15:117–125.

Helfer R.E., Kempe C.H. (eds.). (1992). The Battered Child. Chicago, The University of Chicago Press, 1968.

Herman J.: Trauma and Recovery. New York, Basic Books.

Horowitz K, Weine S, Jekel J. (1995). PTSD symptoms in urban adolescent girls: compounded community trauma. J Am Acad Child Adolesc Psychiatry, 34, 10: 1353–1361.

Hossain Z, Field T, Gonzales J, Malphurs J et al. (1994). Infants of depressed mothers interact better with their non-depressed fathers. Infant Mental Health Journal, 15:348–357.

Khanobdee C, Sukratanachaiyakul V, Gay JT. (1993). Couvade syndrome in expectant Thai fathers. International Journal of Nursing Studies, 30:125–131.

Kitzinger S. (1992). Birth and violence against women generating hypotheses from women's accounts of unhappiness after childbirth. In: Roberts H (Ed.): Women's health matters. Routledge, London, pp. 63–80.

Krug E.G., Dahlberg L.L., Mercy J.A., Zwi A.B., Lozano R. (eds.). (2002). World report on violence and health. Geneva, World Health Organisation.

Lazarus RS. (1969). Patterns of adjustment and human effectiveness. McGraw Hill, New York.

Levy T.M., Orlans M. (2000). Attachment disorder as an antecedent to violence and antisocial patterns in children. In: T.M. Levy (ed.): Handbook of attachment interventions. San Diego, Academic Press.

Levy T.M., Orlans M. (1998). Attachment, trauma, and healing. Understanding and Treating Attachment Disorder in Children and Families. Washington DC, CWLA.

Lyons S. (1998). Post-traumatic stress disorder following childbirth: causes, prevention and treatment. In: Clement S (Ed): Psychological perspectives on pregnancy and childbirth. Churchill Livingstone, Edinburgh, pp. 123–143.

McGee H. et al. (2002). The SAVI report. Dublin. Liffey.

Niven C. (1985). How helpful is the presence of the husband at childbirth? Journal of Reproductive and Infant Psychology, 3:45–53.

Palkovitz R. (1987). Fathers' motives for birth attendance. Maternal-Child Nursing Journal, 16:123–129.

Panksepp J. (1998). The Affective Neuroscience. Oxford, Oxford University Press.

Raphling DL, Carpenter BL, Davis A. (1967). Incest - A genealogical study. Arch Gen Psychiatry 16:505–511.

Rich P. (2006). Attachment and Sexual Offending. Understanding and Applying Attachment Theory to the Treatment of Juvenile Sexual Offenders. Chichester, John Wiley.

Rodgers C.S., Lang A.J., Twamley E.W., Stein M.B. (2003). Sexual trauma and pregnancy. Journal of Woman's Health, 12(10):961–970.

Russel D. (1983). The incidence and prevalence of interfamilial and extrafamilial sexual abuse of female children. Child Abuse and Neglect 7: 133–146.

—. (1986). The secret trauma: incest in the lives of girls and women. New York, Basic Books.

Stolle Dennis P. (2000).Wexler David B., Winick Bruce J. (eds.): Practicing Therapeutic Jurisprudence. Law as a Helping Profession. Durham, Carolina Academic Press.

Office of the United Nations High Commissioner for Human Rights: Legislative History of the Convention on the Rights of the Child. New York and Geneva, United Nations, 2007.

Van der Hart O., Nijenhuis E., Steele K. (2006). The Haunted Self. Structural Dissociation and the Treatment of Chronic Traumatization. New York, W.W. Norton.

Wheatley SL, Brugha TS, Shapiro DA. (2003). Exploring and enhancing engagement to the psychosocial intervention <Preparing for parenthood>. Arch Womens Ment Health, 6:275–285.

CHAPTER TEN

EMPATHY AND EMPOWERMENT: THE FRUITS OF FAMILY LIFE

VICTORIA W. THORESEN

The purpose of family life

From a biological perspective, humans increase the chances of survival for their species by caring for their young as long as they do. Providing food, clothing, and shelter helps ensure the existence of future generations. Caring for, defending, sheltering, feeding, and educating one's offspring is seen to be a natural motivation associated with functioning in a physical environment and as being an instinctive reaction to possible threats or practical necessities. Thus, the fundamental task of family life has been seen by many (Wynn & Coolidge, 2004) as making sure that the basic physical needs of its members are met. However, others (James, 1890, Maslow & Lowery, 1998) have recognized that humans are not only animals but have psychological, social, and spiritual needs as well. With the support of norms and cultural traditions transferred through religion, politics, social conventions, and so on, families have been able to transfer attitudes, knowledge, and competences that help children to function in life.

But physical and social environments change, and as Teilhard de Chardin states: "In the passage of time, a state of collective human consciousness has progressively evolved which is inherited by each succeeding generation of conscious individuals, and to which each generation adds something." (Chardin, 1959) Families not only meet their members' basic needs but also contribute to social change and to the evolution of a collective human consciousness. Families are also faced with the task of sharing elements of the existing collective human consciousness with their members.

The evolution of collective consciousness

Historian Arnold Toynbee claimed that changes in civilization were due to humans' responses to their social and physical environment and are, therefore, an expression of human understanding of the principles underlying existence. (Toynbee, 1961) Pitirim Sorokin built upon Toynbee's ideas by developing a theory of immanent change in which the dominant cultures were "ideational" (value-driven, spiritually focused) rather than "sensate" (favoring empirical evidence and a practical, materialistic way of life). (Sorokin, 1967) Ideational cultures arose from "internal forces" resulting from the integration of peoples' understanding of principles in everyday situations. Social movements, whether they took on the visage of resistance or revolution, or were of limited reformative nature, have always had an ideological foundation regardless of the material manifestations of the ideology. Cries of "Liberté" were accompanied by "Give us bread!" Demands for equality were the motivating force behind pleas to "Free the slaves!" Value-driven internal forces are seen by many to be as powerful, if not more powerful, than external ones. "Material culture is a physical reflection of one's principles and spiritual beliefs." (Miller, 1995). The way people sing and dance, eat, build houses, dispose of waste, establish relationships, wage wars, or build civilizations—all these and more indicate in a million ways what is deemed right or wrong, just or unjust, honorable or dishonorable, achievable or impossible, sustainable or extravagant, compassionate or hedonistic, purposeful and meaningful.

Understanding universal principles

Purpose and meaningfulness are contingent upon the social contracts which emerge from a society's understanding of how the universe functions. With the increased recognition of the complexity and interdependency of systems, insights have emerged concerning the principles determining both material and nonmaterial dimensions of existence. A re-examination of present social contracts requires reflection on these new insights, some of which can be briefly described as follows (Bahai, 1982):

- *Connectivity and cohesion:* This principle refers to a power of attraction which holds atoms together, which keeps plants and animals as distinct beings, and which causes societies to cooperate rather than immediately kill each other off. When the power of connectivity and cohesion is lacking, disintegration occurs and the mineral or plant or animal or civilization, as we know it, collapses. This power of attraction has been called many things: love, the life force, solidarity, and so on. Without connectivity and cohesion, coexistence and collaboration do not exist. Some social scientists refer to connectivity and cohesion in the social world as empathy (Rifkin, 2009)The first place a child experiences connectivity and cohesion is in the family.

- *Transference and transmutation:* This principle refers to the processes of change and augmentative power of growth. There are universal processes of change and growth: minerals are absorbed into the life of a plant; a plant loses its life into that of an animal; an animal becomes a part of humans when it is eaten. Seen in terms of existing natural and social systems, one can recognize these transformations as having to do with growth, adaptation, and evolution—processes which occur naturally in a family**.** In a wider social context, this can be understood as being a social learning process which develops collective knowledge and action.
- *Finiteness:* This principle refers to the recognition of mortality and the existence of immortality. There are limits to growth, resource abundance/scarcity, planetary boundaries, life and death, and civilizations that exist and some that become extinct. Acknowledging and accepting the finiteness of resources, of time and space, contribute to our ability to manage the use of resources. Within a family context, finiteness finds expression in relation to time, economics, energy, and much more.

Crisis of values

Values express our understanding of the underlying principles of existence, and social values are goals towards which behavior moves (Swartz and Bardi, 2001). Throughout the history of human civilization, the way people have understood the principles underlying existence has changed and evolved. Thus, the meanings attributed to values have also varied among individuals and societies. Composite, overarching values such as justice and integrity have been fundamental, but the manner in which they have been exercised has been as diverse as the cultures. Core values such as honesty, trustworthiness, compassion, respect, generosity, excellence, diligence, commitment, humility, patience, courage, and so on, have motivated leaders and individuals but in extremely different ways. Related values, which are dependent on core values and are often the result of basic ethical attitudes, have led to expressions of joyfulness, contentment, kindness, politeness, reliability, flexibility, forgiveness, and so on, all in a multiplicity of forms. It is in the family circle that children learn about values and adopt or reject them.

In the light of the increasing globalization and commercialization of the human race, with global industry and trade, tourism, migration, instant communication, greater tolerance and respect, as well as intensified fears of nuclear destruction, of climate change, of pandemics, of terror actions—there appears to be a degeneration of traditional interpretations of the values which influence how individuals, families, local, national and global communities function. "Our age is widely held to be experiencing a crisis of values…We have lost our ethical bearings and are unable to discern a horizon towards which to move," claims Koichiro Matsuura, former UNESCO Director-General. (Bindé, ed.,2004) As Jerome Bindé states: "The contemporary crisis of values affects not only the traditional moral frameworks transmitted by the great religious faiths but also the secular values that succeeded them (science, progress, the emancipation of peoples, and humanist ideals of solidarity)…We are being compelled to rethink totally the social contracts that underpin our societies." (Bindé, ed.,2004) As Robert Engelman states in the 2013 State of the World Report, "Our predicament at least presents us with opportunity. In the words of poet W. H. Auden, 'We must love one another or die.'" In order to survive, we may find ourselves dragged, kicking and screaming, into ways of relating to each other and the world around that humanity has been aspiring to achieve since the emergence of the great ethical and spiritual traditions many centuries ago." (Engelman, 2013)

Empathy in familiar and global contexts

Empathy is a value which has had its home in the family for centuries. The family has been there, beside each other, together in the same room. They could see each other's tears, hear each other's sighs, and feel each other's pain. They could develop empathy for each other. Empathy and social awareness are primarily aspects of individual behavioral development which are fostered first and foremost in the family.

Jean-Jacques Rousseau stated that empathy springs from compassion and is: "a natural feeling, which, by moderating the violence of love of self in each individual, contributes to the preservation of the whole species." (Rousseau, 1762) Stanley I. Greenspan maintains that a child's development of a self-conscious identity is totally dependent on the empathic relationship between parents and child. (Greenspan & Benderly. 1997) Such relationships consist of concern, compassion, and commitment. Martin L. Hoffmann goes even further, explaining how "the child's innate predisposition for empathic engagement is manifested at each stage of the maturation process, providing the individual with the emotional and cognitive foundation to become a fully formed social being." (Hoffmann, 2000)

Empathy is a constructive response, linking individuals and groups. Empathy is a composite of concern, compassion, and commitment. (Thoresen, 2012). Concern, in this context, refers to a human behavior on the axis between curiosity and anxiety. Concern lies beyond observation, but before insecurity. It encompasses the ability to identify difficulties (such as the planetary boundaries of our environment or the lack of equitable distribution of resources and wealth), the active willingness to get involved, competence in collecting and applying information and data and the ability to envision potential consequences and outcomes. Compassion is an emotional capacity (the cornerstone of humanism and religious traditions), and is considered more vigorous than sympathy. It gives rise to an active desire to alleviate others' suffering. Compassion lies on the axis between sympathy and revenge. It is beyond mere recognition but before hatred. It is based on awareness of the interrelatedness of all—should one suffer injustice, hunger, and so on, then it affects us all ("There, but for fortune, go you or I"). Compassion is also the ability to identify with the human reactions of others in given situations and the willingness to be of service, selflessly involved, or even to sacrifice for others. Empathy also contains aspects of commitment. Commitment is the keeping of a promise, the holding of a contract or vow. Commitment lies on the axis between suggestions and implementation. It is beyond intentions, but before fanaticism. Commitment involves honesty with oneself and others, accountability, determination, creativity, courage, endurance, and patience. Immanuel Kant suggested that promises should always be kept, while some consequentialists argue that promises should be broken whenever doing so would yield benefits. It is in the tension between these two perspectives that moral decisions are made. In a world where fragmentation and separatism were once the norm, the cohesive power of empathy may prove to be a key factor, leading to more unified, cooperative action on the part of the individual as well as on the part of institutions and nations.

Some researchers, such as Jeremy Rifkin, claim that empathy is inherent to human civilization and that globalization has served as a catalyst which has contributed to the development of empathy and its increased role in the modern world. Human civilization, when examined from an historical meta-perspective, can be said to have evolved over centuries from small self-contained units to a large system of interdependent groups. The intimacy of globalization and modern telecommunications has expanded the threshold of our awareness of how others exist and our role in their conditions.

> "...Our quest for universal belonging has catapulted us into ever more complex social and economic arrangements, each of which has pushed out and filled up more of the globe upon which we live. We now have colonized virtually every square inch of the planet and established the scaffolding for a truly global civilization that is connecting the human race in a single embrace, but at the expense of an entropic bill that is threatening our extinction. Through all of the great stages of human history—forager/hunter, hydraulic agriculture, and the First, Second, and emerging Third Industrial Revolutions—human consciousness expanded to encompass the complex energy/communications structures we created. Mythological consciousness, theological consciousness, ideological consciousness, psychological consciousness, and now dramaturgical consciousness mark the evolutionary passages of the human psyche. And with each successive reorientation of consciousness, empathic sensibility reached new heights. But the increasing complexity of human social arrangements also came with greater stresses and more terrifying implosions, especially when the strains produced by increasing differentiation and individuation came up against the demands for increasing integration into the new complex systems we created." (Rifkin, 2009)

Scientists disagree as to whether similar stages of empathic development exist in relation to groups as large as nation-states. From Adam Smith onwards, many voices claim that the loyalties and responsibilities of a government to its citizens demand a prioritizing of initiatives and potential "trade-offs" in favor of the country's own well-being. However, never before has the large majority of people in the world been embedded in the complexly interconnected infrastructures and interactions of modern society. Never before has money, food, products, and information moved across the globe 24 hours a day. Never before have so many travellers, workers, even germs, been transported from one corner of the planet to the other. Never before have so many people lived beyond the constrictions of fighting for survival. And never before has humanity faced such extensive destruction of the environment and the consequences this has on their very existence. These new conditions have expanded the individual's realm of contact and experience and have also contributed to the development of empathy as a significant element determining behavior. Jeremy Rifkin states: "empathy becomes the thread that weaves an increasingly differentiated and individualized population into an integrated social tapestry, allowing the social organism to function as a whole." (Rifkin, 2009)

The role of family

Above and beyond the fulfilment of basic physical needs, the family has the role of transmitting values based on collective understanding of universal principles and promoting the expression of these values through daily actions in the home. Stimulating empathy, based on the recognition of the inherent cohesion and connectivity binding existence, is a fundamental obligation of the family. Doing this by fostering attitudes of sharing, caring, and cooperating creates unity within the family unit. Promoting aspirations of living responsibly and sustainably sets the stage for initiatives which, when combined with those of other individuals, groups, businesses, and governments, can significantly affect the direction of global development. To achieve this, families need to motivate its members to acquire and use core life skills as defined by UNESCO and the WHO in 1994. These core life skills are:

- being able to make decisions
- seeing alternatives and solving problems
- thinking creatively
- thinking critically
- developing communicational competence
- establishing and maintaining social relationships
- knowing oneself
- developing empathy
- managing ones' own emotions
- relating to social change.

In this way, individuals will become empowered to contribute to a more just and equitable society. "Individuals are never more themselves, never more masters of their own fate than when they recognize that they are a part of a greater whole from which they can draw inspiration and strength, and to which they can give inspiration and strength." (Nunn, 1920) Developing a profound sense of responsibility for one's family, the fate of the planet, and for the well-being of the *entire* human family is a first step toward releasing the resources necessary for sustainable human development.

References

Baha'i, The Universal House of Justice. (1982). *Promulgation of Universal Peace,* Bahai Publishing Trust of the United States.

Bindé, Jerome (ed). (2004). *The Future of Values*; UNESCO publishing Berghahn Books, NY Paris.

Engelman, Robert. (2013). "Beyond Sustainable", *Is Sustainability Still Possible?* State of the World Report 2013, Island Press, Washington.

Greenspan, Stanley I. and Beryl Lieff Benderly. (1997). The Growth of the Mind: And the Endangered Origins of Intelligence. Reading. M.A: Addison-Wesley.

Hoffmann, Martin L. (2000). Empathy and Moral Development: Implications for Caring and Justice. NY, Cambridge University Press,. Quoted in The Empathic Civilization p.110.

James, W. (1890). The Principles of Psychology, New York, Henry Holt and Company, vol. 1; Maslow, A.H., (1954), Motivation and Personality, Maslow Publications (available online); Maslow, A.H. and Lowery, R., (1998), Toward a psychology of being, 3rd edition, New York, Wiley & Sons.

Miller, Daniel. (1995). *Acknowledging Consumption;* Routledge Pub. London.

Nunn, Percy. (1920). Education: Its Data and First Principles; Arnold and Co., London.

Rifkin, Jeremy. (2009). *The Empathic Civilization*; Penguin Group Publishers, NYC. P.37.

Rousseau, Jean-Jacques. (1762). Translated to English; Wayne, William Harold, 1907, D. Appelton and co., NYC.

Sorokin, Pitirim. (1967) "Casual, functional and meaningful integration" in Demerath, N.J and Peterson, Richard A.(eds); "*System, Change and Conflict*" N.Y. Free Press.

Swartz, S.H. and Bardi, A. (2001). Value Hierarchies Across Culture in Journal of Cross Cultural Psychology, Vol 32, No. 3, pp 268–290.

Teilhard de Chardin, The Future of Man, (1959) Editions de Seiul, Doubleday, (1964) p. 33.

Thoresen, Victoria. (2012). "Concern, Compassion and Commitment"; *Beyond Consumption, Pathways to Responsible Living;* www.perlprojects.org; Berlin.

Toynbee, Arnold J; 1961, *A Study of History*, Oxford University Press.

Wynn, T. and Coolidge, F., (2004), The Expert Neanderthal Mind, Journal of Human Evolution, Vol. 46, pp.467–487.

STATEMENTS AND DECLARATIONS

Twelfth International Conference & Third World Congress
of Service and Research Foundation of Asia on Family and Culture
(SERFAC), Chennai, India

"Giving Children a Voice: The Transforming Role of the Family in a Global Society"

ORGANIZER

Service and Research Foundation of Asia on Family and Culture (SERFAC), Chennai, India
(An International NGO in Special Consultative Status with ECOSOC of the United Nation, New York)

Statement of Eric Olson

Focal Point, Programme on the Family
Division for Social Policy and Development
United Nations Department of Economic and Social Affairs

Ladies and Gentlemen,

I have been requested by Ms. Elsa Stamatopoulou, Acting Director of the Division for Social Policy and Development at the United Nations Department of Economic and Social Affairs in New York, to deliver the following message on her behalf:

"It gives me great pleasure to send my greetings and warm wishes to all the participants in this Service and Research Foundation of Asia on Family and Culture (SERFAC) World Congress on Children and Family.

I wish to thank SERFAC for hosting and organizing this World Congress on Children and Family, which takes place in view of the twentieth anniversary of the United Nations Convention on the Rights of the Child. The world has also just recently marked, in December 2008, the sixtieth anniversary of the Universal Declaration of Human Rights, in which the family was recognized as the natural and fundamental group unit of society, entitled to protection by society and the state.

It is our hope that the observance of these anniversaries will provide a renewed and continued impetus for all partners—governments, civil society, the private sector and the United Nations system—to come together and reaffirm our global commitment to the well-being of children and the family, which play such a vital role in our work for development and peace.

As we begin the New Year 2009, the world continues to be marked by change and transformation, including upheaval and crisis, on an increasingly globalized level. In such a world, the task of promoting the well-being of children and families is more important than ever. I wish to warmly congratulate SERF AC for working to fulfil this mission."

Having delivered this message, I wish to add, on my own behalf, as Focal Point for the United Nations Programme on the Family, that it is a pleasure for me to be here to address this SERFAC World Congress. I would like to thank Dr. Bernard, the International Programme Planning Core Committee, and everyone involved with the planning and organizing of this World Congress for their extensive preparations and for their warm hospitality. I am extremely grateful to Dr. Bernard and SERFAC for their wonderful support to, and partnership with, the Programme on the Family over the past several years.

I wish to start my remarks by considering the concept of "Family." Each of us belongs to a family, and each of us has our own very personal understanding of Family. Families provide nurturing, care, and support to their members, who enjoy a sense of identity, affiliation, and responsibility, even when these individual members may not be living together under one roof. As individuals we have a basic human need to receive this support, and to provide it to other members of our family.

Family networks have been a pillar of societies for centuries. Adults provided care to children who in turn provided care to them in their old age. The networks ensured that the needs of the family and of the individuals within the family were taken care of by, and within, the family. Families delivered a form of social services and provided social protection, providing for their members during times of stress, such as financial hardship, or family tragedy, such as caring for children after the premature death of a parent.

More recently, the Family has undergone profound transformations. Average family size has decreased all over the world; young people are getting married at a later age; more women work outside the home; the average age of mothers at first birth has increased; infant mortality rates have declined; and couples are having fewer children; and average life expectancy continues to increase. The traditional, large extended family is being replaced by the smaller nuclear family, even as grandparents are living longer and several family generations are living side by side.

Alternative forms of union have grown more common, such as unmarried cohabitation, or spouses in married couples not living in the same village, city, or country due to migration for work. Divorce has increased, accompanied by remarriage, with more and more children living in a family with a step-parent. Significant numbers of single-parent families and single-person households have emerged, including a rising number of older persons living alone. And, in many countries, the HIV/AIDS pandemic is wreaking havoc on families, straining them to take care of sick family members, with the whole family often under a dark cloud of social stigma, and depriving children of their parents, leaving grandparents or older siblings to care for younger children.

Some of the changes in family have brought new opportunities, such as new and wider choices, increased empowerment, and improved status for girls and women. However, many of these transformations also call into question the effect that they may be having on our children, as well as the structure of society as we know it. They challenge our thinking about family, and they require us to work together to face family problems. They also challenge us to adapt, shape, and reshape public policy in ways that address the needs of families, to ensure that basic services such as education and health are provided to all citizens—especially children.

Over the years, families in Asia, who are known for being remarkably strong and resilient, as well as families around the world, have experienced many pressures and numerous challenges. Due to economic factors, family members—often males, but also increasingly females—have migrated to places of employment, leaving their wives or husbands, children, and parents at home. Worker remittances have proven to be a very important survival strategy for family members at home. In recent decades, migration has become increasingly international, and today many Asian families have members living in other countries on the continent or overseas.

Through all of these changes, many families have proved highly resilient, able to blend traditional and modem values and practices in order to ensure the survival and development of their members. Other families have experienced these changes with more difficulty. All of these families, both highly resilient and those less so, are in need of additional support—from communities, from civil society, from the private sector, and most of all, from Governments.

Yet the centrality of family often escapes the attention of policy makers. They should be encouraged to give greater thought to the contributions families make to the well-being of their members and of society, and to consider how policies affect families and to integrate a family perspective into policymaking. Policies and programmes that fail to consider families and their children are not likely to offer the necessary support families need. The solution 1S to ensure that policy makers take into account the needs of families and consider how their actions will assist families or hinder them from meeting their needs. Some countries have become increasingly interested in considering how all their policies affect and influence families—both positively and negatively—and some have taken steps to develop and implement national family policies.

The family will continue to be essential for the well-being of children and for human well-being in general. Policies and programmes must recognize this vital role and seek to support it through the integration of a family perspective and through advocacy for family issues, whether at the local, national, or international level. The United Nations Programme on the Family will continue to strive to fulfil this function at the international level, and to promote it at the national level as well.

I look forward to participating in this World Congress and to interacting with you during the next four days.

Thank you

Final Declaration from the participating Children presented to the Plenary Assembly at the conclusion of the Congress on January 7, 2009

Preamble

To grow physically, emotionally, spiritually and intellectually, a child must essentially be happy. Every child has the right to a happy childhood, protected from all sides without any distinction or discrimination on the basis of color, sex, religion, race, nationality or caste. Despite the fact that we come from different nations, speak different languages, practice different religions, our hearts speak as one.

Idealism is an inherent part of every child, which enables us to come up with ingenious and exemplary ideas. However, it is incomplete if we are unable to manifest it into realism. Recognizing that children all over the world are living in exceptionally difficult conditions, core issues like poverty, illiteracy, gender disparities and violence are insufficiently and ineffectively dealt with. The World Congress facilitated a genesis of ideas which transcends all social, geographical, economic, religious and cultural barriers. Thus, we the Children of the World hereby declare:

Resolutions

- Governments should pass legislations that promote and prioritize the requirements of children and childhood, in particular their education and safety and ensure strict implementation
- Restructuring of the syllabi to a more relevant and contemporary curriculum
- Promotion of life skills through experiential learning and better counselling programmes
- Devising global laws against agents of child trafficking and stricter enforcements of preventive measures such as sealing of borders, and cooperation between source countries and destination countries
- The Governments and its allied organizations must ensure the rescue and rehabilitation of victims of child trafficking, child prostitution, sexual abuse, drug abuse and exploitation at proper age and time
- Functional trauma centers must be set up to give paramedical and psychological care and help to the above mentioned victims
- Children should be totally prohibited from working in hazardous industries like mining, fireworks and heavy duty agriculture

- In situations where children have to work to support family income, they must be above minimum 10 years of age, and their education must not be compromised
- Children need to enjoy the character, love and understanding which must therefore be brought under the auspices of his/her parents under their responsibility, in an atmosphere, of compassion, moral and material security, except in certain circumstances, such as young children separated from their mothers
- Community and public authorities must provide special care for children deprived of family and those people who lack access to subsistence living
- More allocation of the country's GDP towards education.
- Decentralization of administration of education to ensure more accountability and regulation of quality checks.
- Revision of curriculum to include more relevant and contemporary syllabus.
- Re-orientation of textbooks to promote peace, communal harmony.
- Inclusion of value education programmes and experiential learning programmes to promote life skills
- Encourage secular views by acknowledging diversity through celebrating all festivals and inculcating respect for all religions
- Governments should encourage respect for all religions by introducing an interpretation of all religious texts in schools thereby eradicating the misconceptions existing about all religions.

The children of the World Congress acknowledge that the above mentioned problems all stem from the vicious cycle of poverty, illiteracy, deprivation and neglect, which is inescapable and cripples a child for life, rendering him/her inadequately equipped to meet the challenges of life.

The participants of the Congress have identified severing of family and community bonds along with the insufficient implementation and lack of accountability on the part of the responsible bodies, as the reasons for the perpetuation of incumbent issues like child trafficking, child labor, child prostitution, terrorism, sexual abuse, organ trade, etc.

Therefore, we hope that our voice is heard, and the Governments of the world, along with all International Institutions, make amends to address all problems related to children.

Service and Research Foundation of Asia on Family and Culture (SERFAC), Chennai, India (An International NGO in Special Consultative Status with ECOSOC of the United Nation, New York)

World Congress

"Giving Children a Voice: The Transforming Role of the Family in a Global Society"

3–7 January, 2009

Concluding Declaration

(Approved at the plenary on 7 January 2009, 10.00 a.m.)

We, the 140 participants, including 33 children, from 33 countries and six religious traditions, of the 12th International conference of which this is the Third World Congress, on 'Giving Children a Voice: The Transforming Role of the Family in a Global Society,' organized by SERFAC (Service and Research Foundation of Asia on Family and Culture) at New Delhi, on 3–7 January 2009, declare unequivocally the primacy and centrality of the Family in caring for and nurturing all children for a healthy future. We are deeply concerned to note that the functions of the family are taken over by commercial and social institutions. Therefore family is not at the centerstage of governance or policy making. We are painfully aware that the unequal distribution of power and the world's resources, ominous forces of war, terrorism, violence, globalization, migration, rapid urbanization, pollution of the environment and mind, corruption and weak governance are negatively impacting the lives of children and families. Technology which has revolutionized the century in many positive ways has also in its inappropriate use contributed to the breakdown of marriage and family leading to the dehumanization and commodification of children through various ways including pornography and abusive images of children. Having heard the voices of children from India, Iraq, Lebanon, Nepal, Pakistan, Palestine, Rwanda, Syria, and United States, we are rudely awakened by their cries for care, love, justice, security and a sustainable future and a voice for them.

Recognizing the importance of the Millennium Development Goals, the recommendations of the General Assembly (2006), and the Convention on the Rights of the Child, including the two optional protocols (2006), we strongly believe that the following initiatives should be undertaken on an urgent basis to enable the family to exercise its transforming role:

1. Promote a family-based and family-centered approach to development and the empowerment of families, since large number of violations of child rights takes place within the families.
2. Reflect on attitudes, belief systems and practices that require change within our own families.
3. Engage Governments, United Nations, regional bodies like SAARC, Civil Society organizations, Religious institutions, Media, Private Sector, Research and Academic institutions and local communities to adopt family-centered policies and advocate the well-being of families and children.
4. Advocate educational systems that promote human dignity and universal values.
5. Integrate peace and justice into the school curriculum starting with early education that draws upon the spiritual principles common to world religions.
6. Raise awareness of the public on gender-related issues and children's rights.
7. Take measures to prevent all forms of child abuse and to adopt intervention measures to assist the victims.
8. Recommend systems of restorative justice for child and youth offenders.
9. Educate children to protect themselves from abuse.
10. Protect children from the negative impact of migration through pre-departure seminars, care giving workshops and support groups for parents, guardians and other stakeholders in collaboration with non-profit organizations, church groups, and others.
11. Train children in resiliency skills to strengthen them in the face of adversity.
12. Promote responsible use of technologies, with urgent attention to the internet, television and mobile communications, based on human values, respect for self and others and child rights.
13. Search for a just world through an on-going inter -faith and inter-cultural dialogue of life.
14. Give children their own public voice through activities such as 'children's parliaments' and clubs, so that they also become agents of change.
15. Encourage the print and electronic media to give more space to children and their concerns through responsible programming and publication.
16. Develop holistic health care for children and families.

We strongly urge:

- Local and National Governments, the United Nations and its institutions, and International Organizations to make family and children the center of their policy making and laws.
- Private Sector to initiate family-friendly employment policies and practices.
- Research and academic institutions to give higher priority to curriculum and research on issues related to child protection and families.
- All stakeholders including Civil Society Organizations, Non-Governmental Organizations and religious institutions to implement the initiatives suggested.
- All people to create a caring and nurturing environment conducive to the well-being of family and children.

We thank and commend SERFAC for its commitment to children and family and for organizing this Third world congress on "Giving Children a Voice: The Transforming Role of the Family in a Global Society."

We commit ourselves to an active ongoing process of listening to our children and of creating for them a more humane world.

AUTHOR PROFILES

1. **Dr. Catherine Bernard, M.B.B.S, M.S., India:** Founder-President-Director of Service and Research Institute on Family and Children (SERFAC), Chennai, India, Chairperson of the International Program Planning Committee of the Global Conference and Convener of the International Think Tank Initiatives of SERFAC.

   Dr. Sr. Catherine Bernard belongs to the Congregation of the Sisters of the Cross of Chavanod, France. She is a medical doctor by profession and holds a post graduate degree in Religion and Religious Education from Fordham University, New York. She is a world-renowned speaker, organizer, writer, and consultant on all aspects of family life, from Natural Family Planning to Effective Parenting and Family Spirituality. She is the Founder of the Society of Family Integrity and Development in Tiruchirapalli, South India (founded in 1976) and in 1986 she founded SERFAC.

   She has organized 12 International Conferences (of which three were World Congresses), apart from the Global Conference at Bangkok, Thailand.

   She has given interviews in various countries to the Press and Television, and has traveled extensively in her own country, India, and in other countries of Asia, Europe, Australia, Africa and the Americas, promoting the stability of marriage and the well-being of families.

2. **Dr. Caroline S. de Leon, Ph.D., Philippines:** Dean of the College of Education and Chairperson of the Guidance and Counselling Department at Miriam College, Philippines.

   Dr. Caroline S. de Leon has an M.A. in Family Life Education and a Ph.D. in Child and Family Studies. A member of the training team of the UNESCO-Asia Pacific Network for International Education and Values Education (APNIEVE-

Philippines), she conducts teacher-training workshops on values across the curriculum for both public and private school teachers throughout the Philippines. She has conducted seminars for teachers, parents and religious communities on family issues, values education, parenting, and human development.

3. **Dr. H. B. Danesh, MD., FRCP., Canada:** Founder and president of the International Education for Peace Institute (Canada and Switzerland). He is a retired professor of conflict resolution and peace education and psychiatry. His areas of research and expertise include peace studies, peace-based education, peace-based leadership, religion and peace, causes and prevention of violence, marriage and family therapy, unity-based conflict resolution, and psychology of spirituality. Dr. Danesh is the author and creator of the internationally acclaimed Education for Peace Program – first piloted in Bosnia and Herzegovina – and the main author of its multivolume curriculum.

4. **Dr. M. K. George S J, Ph.D., India:** Director, Indian Social Institute, Bengaluru. He is also Research Guide, University of Kerala. He served as a member of the faculty and honorary Director, Loyola Extension Services, between 1986 and 2009. He was on the Faculty, Sociology Department, Loyola College of Social Sciences. from 1989 to 2008 and was the Principal, Loyola College of Social Sciences, from 2004 to 2008. He was also International Visiting Fellow, College of the Holy Cross, Worcester, MA, USA (2008–2009).

   His publications include Development Induced Displacement. (Co-author) 2003, Chapter on Paulo Freire, Participatory Development for Water (Co-author) 2009 and Human Development Approach to Access to Income: Case Study of NREGA (Co-author).

5. **Dr. Ethel Quayle, Ph.D., Scotland:** Senior Lecturer in Clinical Psychology, School of Health in Social Science, University of Edinburgh, and Director, COPINE Research.

   Dr. Ethel Quayle is a clinical psychologist and course director for adult mental health, with a specialist interest in Cognitive Behavior Therapy. For the past twelve years, she has been working in the area of Internet abuse images. She has published widely in this area. Dr. Quayle is a member of the Home Office Task Force on Internet Safety.

6. **Professor Max Taylor, Ph.D., Scotland:** Professor Taylor was Professor of Applied Psychology, University College, Cork, Ireland, from 1983 to 2006, and subsequently Director at the Centre for the Study of Terrorism and Political Violence in the International Relations University of St. Andrews. He is a visiting Professor, Department of Security and Crime Sciences, University College, London and a legal and forensic psychologist with wide international experience of research and consultancy in the area of terrorism and terrorist behavior. He holds consultancies for Government and private companies, and does legal and forensic court work. He is Editor of the journal *Terrorism and Political Violence.*

7. **Dr. John Shea, Ph.D., MSW, USA:** Retired Professor of the Practise of Pastoral Care and Counseling, in The School of Theology and Ministry, Boston College, Massachusetts, USA.

   Dr. Shea has over 30 years' experience in the field of counseling. He is an international lecturer and speaker, and has authored several books and numerous articles that focus on Spirituality, Experiencing, and Adulthood.

8. **Prof. Victoria Wyszynski Thoresen, Norway:** Associate Professor of Education at the Hedmark University College, Norway, and Project Manager of the Consumer Citizenship Network.

   Prof. Thoresen has specialized in curriculum development, global education, peace education, value-based education, lifelong learning, and consumer education. In addition to many years of experience as a teacher and teacher-trainer, she has written textbooks for schools and teacher training and has functioned as an international educational consultant. She has assisted UNEP and the UN Marrakech Process Task Forces in the development of a core curriculum for education for sustainable consumption. She has functioned as an international expert contributing to the creation of International Standards (26000) for Social Responsibility and has also been appointed UNESCO Chair for Education for Sustainable Lifestyles.

9. **Dr. Werner Tschan, M.D.**: A practising psychiatrist based in Basel, Switzerland. He holds three academic degrees – MD, Master in Applied Ethics, and a Certificate in the treatment of sexual offenders. He is the author of the book titled Prof*essional Sexual Misconduct in Institutions: Causes and Consequences, Prevention and Intervention.* He is dedicated to preventing violence. He has written several articles and has been lecturing worldwide on this subject. His publications are available in English, German, French, and Japanese. He participated in the German Round Table on Prevention of Sexual Abuse and is a member of the advisory board of advocateweb. He provides solutions based on first-hand experience derived from the treatment of numerous survivors of violence and their relatives and also of offender-professionals, besides understanding gained as a consultant in various institutions.

10. **Dr. John Wall, Ph.D., USA**: Professor of Religion and Childhood Studies at Rutgers University, Camden, United States. He is the author of *Children's Rights: Today's Global Challenge* (forthcoming), *Ethics in Light of Childhood* (2010) and *Moral Creativity* (2005), co-editor of *Children and Armed Conflict* (2011), *Marriage, Health, and the Professions* (2002), and *Paul Ricoeur and Contemporary Moral Thought* (2002), and numerous articles on ethical theory, religion, postmodernism, children's political participation, and children's rights.

11. **Dr. Janis Wolak, J.D., USA**: Senior Researcher at the Crimes against Children Research Center of the University of New Hampshire, United States. She is the author and co-author of numerous articles about child victimization and technology-facilitated child sexual exploitation crimes. She has conducted several U.S. national research projects about the characteristics and dynamics of child sexual exploitation crimes, which have been funded by the US Department of Justice and the National Science Foundation